MODERN ENGLISH GRAMMAR

the Title of

MODERN ENGLISH GRAMMAR

First published November 2019
Written by Seunghyun Baek (Ph.D),
Chonnam National University
Publisher: Byung-Seok Jeong
ISBN 978-89-6849-672-1 (93740)
Price: 18,000 Won

Published by Chonnam National University Press,
77 Yongbong-ro, Bukgu, Gwangju,
Republic of Korea, 61186
Tel: 82-62-530-0571/3, Fax: 82-62-530-0579

Printed and bound in the Republic of Korea

CIP No : CIP2019046842

MODERN ENGLISH GRAMMAR

Seunghyun Baek

CHONNAM NATIONAL UNIVERSITY **PRESS**

Preface

The objective of this book is to help English as a foreign language (EFL) or a second language (ESL) learners and teachers understand the fundamentals of English grammar that are most frequently and commonly used in an academic context. This text covers the following: (1) Tense (Present; Past; Future), (2) Aspect (Present Perfect; Past Perfect; Future Perfect), (3) Auxiliary (Modal) Verb, (4) Passive, (5) Determiner and Noun, (6) Pronoun, (7) Subject-Verb Agreement, (8) Infinitive, (9) Gerund, (10) Clause (Noun; Adjectival; Adverbial), and (11) Hypothetical If.

I wish first to thank Hyunwook Kim and Jiyoung Park, who supported me to edit this valuable text. Last but not least, I am grateful to my wife, Kwangsun Hwang and my son, Jonmin Baek whose patience and love was almost endless during the writing of this English edition.

Contents

1
PRESENT

1.1 Introduction

Present Tenses

There are two types of present tenses in English verb. One is 'simple present' or 'present simple,' and the other is 'present progressive' or 'present continuous.' Forms of 'simple present' or 'present simple' are like *I sleep, she memorizes.* Forms of 'present progressive' or 'present continuous' are like *I am sleeping or she's memorizing.* The two present tenses function in multiple ways.

Simple Present

The simple present tense can refer to something that regularly exists or habitually happens. This tense is used to talk about states or actions in the present and it sometimes refers to general truths.

Present Progressive

The present progressive tense can express a state or action in progress in the present time.

1.2 Usage

Simple Present

1) The simple present tense can state general/scientific facts or the way things exist.

ex) Water boils at 100° Celsius.
The earth moves around the sun.

2) The simple present tense can be used to talk about the activities which occur regularly (i.e., daily, weekly or monthly). This tense is used to talk about what routinely happens.

ex) She eats out every Sunday night.
I visit my grandparents every weekend.

3) The simple present tense can express activities for custom or habit. This tense represents relatively permanent situations.

ex) This tradition bonds one generation to the next one.
We eat locally produced vegetables.

4) The simple present is used to talk about a future situation, such as *a scheduled event and time-table activity.*

ex) The train arrives in London at 6 p.m.
The school term begins on September 1st.

5) The simple present tense can be used to talk about the future in time-clauses following the conjunctions such as *before, after, until, as soon as* or *when* and in conditional if-clauses following the conjunctions such as *if* or *unless.*

ex) If Real Madrid wins tomorrow, they will be champions.
I will buy some ice creams before she arrives.

Present Progressive

1) The present progressive tense is used to express an observation of the action which is happening at the point, the momentary change, or the moment of speaking.

ex) Snow is falling on my head.
The ice is melting now.

2) The present progressive tense can represent not routine and regular states but short-term and temporary activities which are just happening at that moment.

ex) I'm reading a lot these days.
We are renovating our roof this week.

3) When present progressive tense is used with *all the time, always or continually,* this tense can be used to describe annoyance which expresses and emphasizes a continuous sequence of repeated behaviors.

ex) She is always breaking something.
They are quarreling all the time.
He is always being late.

4) The present progressive tense can be used to talk about something that is occurring earlier and later than a given time.

ex) At six o'clock we are usually having dinner.
While the children are sleeping. I usually do the dishes

5) The present progressive is used to talk about a future situation, such as *a personal arrangement and planned activity.*

ex) I'm meeting my girlfriend tonight.
We're having a party tomorrow. Would you like to come?

1.3 Static vs. Dynamic Verbs

A static (linking) verb (i.e., belong, hear, realize, and see) describes a state of being, sensation or perception. Therefore, this verb mostly takes the non-progressive form. However, a dynamic verb represents an action and activity which we carry out and thus this verb can be the progressive form.

ex) The pasta tastes too salty. (static)
A dog is chasing him now. (dynamic)

Exercise

A. Put the verbs into the correct form.

1. We (play) basketball once a week.
2. Hurricane winds (blow) from 80 to 140 miles per hour.
3. My mother always (prepare) too much food.
4. The plane (arrive) at 18.00.
5. I (work) to get my teaching certification these days.
6. It will be nice to see John when he (get) home.
7. The sun (set) down the mountains now.
8. I (meet) my grandparents tonight.
9. He usually (drink) coffee at breakfast.
10. The online Korean course (begin) next week.

11. Michael (leave) for Paris this evening.

12. My grandmother (believe) in life after death.

13. The runners of the marathon (approach) the finish line now.

14. Water (freeze) at zero degrees.

15. Every year my family (go) to Japan for a week.

16. If it (rain) tomorrow, we'll stay at home.

17. My husband (complain) about his work all the time.

18. We (discuss) the solution to the problem now.

19. She usually (have) a regular health checkup.

20. I (work) in New York this month but I will return to Korea next month.

B. Read each sentence and choose the correct answer.

1. Travelling in a spaceship (sounds / is sounding) interesting to me.

2. I can't hear you because the fire station (sounds / is sounding) the fire alarm too loudly. Can you say that again?

3. I'm looking for a soft pillow. So I (feel / am feeling) the material of the pillow to see if it is soft enough.

4. Did you make a decision? Yes, I'll take it. I (feel / am feeling) lucky to have your offer.

5. What are you doing here? I (taste / am tasting) the soup to know whether it has gone bad.

6. How is the food? It (tastes / is tasting) awful. I have to throw it away.

7. Last night, I (heard / listened to) footsteps behind me on my way home.

8. You must have been scared. You had better not (hear / listen to) music with earphones at night.

9. Your room (smells / is smelling) bad. When did you open the windows lastly?

10. I (smell / am smelling) the lilies which my husband bought me yesterday.

2

PAST

2.1 Introduction

Simple Past

The simple past can express many types of past situations or events: singular past events, repeated past activities, and more long-lasting past situations. Besides, the simple past indicates the events, activities, and situations that happened in the past and are finished before the moment of speaking.

Past Progressive

The past progressive can represent situations or events that were going on around a specific past time. In addition, this tense can indicate a past action with repetition as well as background-event interrupted by another past action.

2.2 Usage

Simple Past

1) The simple past tense can state a situation or event that occurred once and ended now.

ex) He told me that before.
I participated in a conference in Tokyo last year.

2) The simple past tense can be used to talk about actions that happened repeatedly or habitually.

ex) We ate out every night last month.
I ran to catch my bus every morning.

3) The simple past tense can express more long-lasting state that ended in the past.

ex) He lived in Seoul for ten years after graduating high school.
I knew him for three years.

Past Progressive

1) The past progressive can be used to express not permanent but temporary situations and events in the past.

ex) Everyone was laughing at the meeting.
John was standing on the subway platform.

2) The past progressive can represent a temporary change from the regular and usual situation.

ex) Alice was commuting to New York for two months.
In June I was working in a department store.

3) The past progressive can be used to indicate gradual growth or change.

ex) The children were growing up quickly.
His hair was going grey.

4) The past progressive can be used to talk about something that was going on around a specific past time.

ex) What were you doing at 11 o'clock yesterday?
I was writing my diary at 8 p.m.

5) When the past progressive is used with a simple past, the past progressive represents a longer background situation or activity; the simple past indicates a shorter event or activity that interrupted the longer situation or activity.

ex) As we were watching television, the phone rang.
I was waiting for the subway when the accident happened.

Exercise

Put the verbs into the correct form.

1. My friends (go) to Chicago two weeks ago.

2. Jane (work) in a shoe shop for a month.

3. I (love) him for a long time but never told that to him.

4. I (call) him three times today, but he didn't answer the phone.

5. My brothers (watch) a movie yesterday at 8 p.m.
   My brothers (watch) a movie yesterday.

6. We (catch) a lot of fish in the river yesterday.

7. I (sleep) when somebody knocked on the door.

8. She (win) a gold medal at the 2018 Winter Olympics.

9. Every weekend I (visit) my grandma during the last winter vacation.

10. Sarah (wait) at the hospital this morning at 10 o'clock.

11. Police (receive) several complaints about the noise last month.

12. I (eat) a bunch of junk food during teenage years.

13. Andrew lost his watch while he (play) basketball.

14. She (spend) her childhood in a small town.

15. She (ask) me personal questions yesterday.

16. We (walk) along the street this time last week.

17. Early humans (live) in caves a long time ago.

18. My family (come) to visit me last January.

19. I (have) a terrible headache yesterday.

20. While Susan (cook), she burnt her finger.

21. I (take) a walk every night to lose weight last year.

22. The Chosun Dynasty era (last) about five centuries.

23. It (snow) outside when she woke up.

24. She (work) at a chocolate factory in 2000.

25. We (go) to the hospital the day before yesterday.

26. I (wait) for you at the cafeteria when you called me.

27. Maris (graduate) from Harvard University last year.

28. Helen Keller (die) at the age of 87.

29. While he (sleep), someone took his wallet.

30. The First World War officially (end) on 3rd October 2010.

31. I (have) dinner with my friends at 7 p.m. yesterday.

32. I (watch) television when the power went out.

3

FUTURE

3.1 Introduction

Simple Future

There are multiple ways to make use of verbs in order to express the future in English. First of all, ***will*** can be used when to present information about the future, or to talk about possible future activities that are not decided yet. ***Will*** can also express a general prediction based on the speaker's belief, intuition or calculation. Additionally, ***be going to*** can refer to planned future events or predictions based on current evidence such as *weather reports or statistical data*. Sometimes, ***simple present*** and ***present progressive*** can also express the future; more specifically, simple present can describe scheduled-events and time-tabled activities. Meanwhile, present progressive can express planned activities and personal arrangements that have already been decided. (see Ch.1, for simple present and present progressive about the future)

Future Progressive

Future progressive can express events or activities that will be going on at a certain time in the future. This tense can also be used to talk about scheduled events and kinds of time table with a specific point in the future.

3.2 Usage

Will

1) ***Will*** can be used to talk about subjective predictions about the future; such predictions are mainly based on not external evidence but one's intuition and personal judgement.

ex) New York Yankees will win a championship because I am a big fan of the team.
I'm not sure, but I think I'll have a break next month.

2) ***Will*** can refer to voluntary behaviors, willingness, or decisions that are made at the moment of speaking. On many occasions, ***Will*** can be used to express a response to someone's request or complaint. In addition, ***Will*** can be used when we ask someone to help do something for us.

ex) Oh, the phone is ringing now. I'll get it.
A: Sorry, I dropped all the cake.
B: Don't worry, I'll clean it up.

3) ***Will*** can express offers or promises.

ex) I'll send you an email.
I promise I will not tell anyone about the surprise party.

Be Going To

1) ***Be going to*** can be used to express future predictions based on present objective evidence such as *statistical data or weather reports*.

ex) The weather forecast says that it's going to rain heavily next week.
Peter is going to win the presidential election based on the preliminary survey.

2) ***Be going to*** can represent prior plans or intentions that have been made at an earlier time. It is not important whether or not the plans are realistic and plausible.

ex) She is going to move to London.
Tom says he's going to become a lawyer.

3) ***Be going to*** can be used to express commands or emphatic rejections.

ex) You're going to take this medicine.
I'm not going to sit up all day listening to your problems.

Future Progressive

1) The future progressive can be used to talk about events or activities that will be going on at a specific time in the future.

ex) We will be thinking of better ways to help you.
This time tomorrow, I'll be swimming in the sea.

2) The future progressive can refer to scheduled events, fixed plans, and expected activities with a certain point in the future.

ex) He will be seeing you anytime soon.
Professor Baek will be giving another lecture on English grammar next week.

3) The future progressive can indicate an ongoing background activity interrupted by another shorter activity in the future.

ex) I will be waiting for you at the bus stop when you arrive.
We will be staying in Sydney by the time he comes back.

4) The future progressive can represent polite inquiries in an indirect manner about one's plans.

ex) Excuse me. Will you be using this pen?
Will you be going to the market this evening?

Exercise

Read each sentence and choose the correct answer.

1. I promise I (will / am going to) send you the contract tomorrow.

2. We (will / are going to) spend our vacation in Spain.

3. Look at that bus! It (will / is going to) crash into a tree.

4. I think Germany (will / is going to) win the World Cup because I can feel it in my bones.

5. You (will not / are not going to) play baseball in my backyard.

6. Somebody is knocking on the door. I (will / am going to) check out who the person is.

7. I (will / am going to) give my mother flowers for her birthday.

8. He (will / is going to) retire at the end of next year.

9. Your bag looks heavy. I (will / am going to) help you until you get home.

10. According to the weather forecast, it (will/ is going to) rain this weekend.

11. A: I'm really hungry.
    B: I (will/ am going to) make some toasts for you.

12. We (will / are going to) buy the train tickets tomorrow.

13. Jennifer (will / is going to) begin medical school next year.

14. You look tired. I (will / am going to) do the dishes for you.

15. I (will / am going to) participate in the workshop tomorrow.

16. I'm sure she (will / is going to) win the first prize because I love her songs.

17. I promise I (will / am going to) help you find a new job.

18. The president (will / is going to) visit France for a world conference next month.

19. The doctor said my sister (will / is going to) have a baby in December.

20. I (will / am going to) clean the house this afternoon if you want me to.

21. When I grow up, I (will / am going to) be a soccer player.

22. He (will / is going to) sell his house as soon as possible.

23. Look out! You (will / are going) to fall off the bike.

B. Put the verb into the correct form.

1. This time tomorrow, we (fly) to France from Denmark.

2. By this time tomorrow, I (write) my essay for a scholarship.

3. We (eat) lunch by the time you arrive.

4. Will you (go) to the cinema this evening?

4
PRESENT PERFECT

4.1 Introduction

Present Perfect

Present perfect can refer to activities that occurred at unspecific past time and just around now or ended recently. In addition, this aspect has a positive or negative effect on the present situation; present perfect is used to make a connection between the present and past. Therefore, this aspect puts more emphasis on a result and duration than on an action itself [Aspect is a grammatical category that represents time-related features (i.e., the completion, duration, or repetition of an action). As a result, aspect is more concerned about how an event or a situation extends over time while tense is more concerned about how time is marked and denoted].

Present Perfect Progressive

Present perfect progressive can express events or situations that have duration and repetition. The events or situations began in the past but perhaps remain unfinished in a certain period of time; as a result, these may possibly be going up to a certain moment of near future.

4.2 Usage

Present Perfect

1) Present perfect can express permanent or long-lasting situations.

ex) I have lived in Korea my whole lifetime.
My father has worked at a law firm for 20 years.

2) Present perfect can be used to talk about finished events or activities that have an impact on the present situation.

ex) I have bought a nice car. (I can give you a ride now.)
He has passed the exam. (He is qualified for the position now.)

3) Present perfect can state life experiences and this can be often used with the words 'never' and 'ever.'

ex) She has visited Singapore three times.

I have never seen a masterpiece of Picasso in person.
This is the first time that I have seen him dance.
It is the second time that we have been to Mexico.

4) Present perfect can be used to express actions that began in the past and lasted up to now. This aspect can be often used with the words 'since' and 'for.'

ex) We have lived in Seattle since 1995.
I haven't had a day off for ten months.
Our traditions have remained constant up to now.

Present Perfect Progressive

1) Present perfect progressive can be used to talk about temporary or short-term situations.

ex) I have been living in my cousin's apartment for two months.
She has been working at a grocery store recently.

2) Present perfect progressive can express ongoing actions and situations that began in the past and are still unfinished and this aspect can indicate repeated actions or activities.

ex) It has been snowing all night. (It's still snowing.)
I have been waiting for him here since 3 p.m. (I'm still waiting.)

4.3 Simple Past vs. Present Perfect

Simple past can be used to indicate something that happened at a specific time in the past and this tense is usually paired with past time expressions (i.e., three weeks ago, in 2018, last year, and yesterday). However, present perfect can be used to express the situations or actions up to now. In other words, events that happened in the past have a link with the present situation. Therefore, this may have a positive or negative impact on the current situation or result. This aspect is often paired with up-to-now time expressions (i.e., in the last seven months, this week, this year, and today). Note that present perfect cannot be used with past time expressions in that the present perfect centers on the present, but the simple past focuses on the past.

ex) I lost my house key yesterday. (There is no information on whether I find it or not now.)
I have lost my house key. (I can't enter my house now.)
I haven't seen Paul today. Do you know where he is? (said to a colleague during the office working hours.)
I didn't see Paul today. Do you know where he was? (said to a colleague on the bus on the way home.)

4.4 Present Perfect vs. Present Perfect Progressive

Present perfect places an emphasis on the duration of situations or activities; they began in a specific past time and lasted or lasts up to the very recent past or now. However, present perfect progressive puts more emphasis on the nature of recurring situations or the activities that have duration and repetition; they began in the past and lasted up to now and went on repetitively or periodically.

ex) I have done my work.
(My work is completed now; the emphasis is placed on the duration and completion of the work.)
I have been doing my work.
(It does not matter whether the work is completed now; the emphasis is placed on the continuous course of doing my work.)

Exercise

Put the verb into the correct form.

1. She (write) a book on the history of art. (You can buy it.)

2. I (try) never to take a trip to Asia in my life.

3. We (work) on this project since 10 o'clock this morning.

4. For 1000 years, the temple (stand) on the mountain.

5. I (enjoy) spending time with my parents since I was a kid.

6. Susan usually works in Toronto but she (work) in Vancouver for the last 2 weeks.

7. We (live) in this house since 1990.

8. The bus already (leave)! What should we do?

9. The football team never (win) a game so far this season.

10. My Spanish really (improve) since I moved to Spain.

11. Robert (play) the violin since he was a little boy.

12. My father (drive) the same car for five years.

13. We (eat) at the Chinese restaurant several times.

14. I (not sleep) all night. (I am feeling tired now.)

15. My sister (work) at a bank since graduating from college.

16. I (know) William since I was born.

17. My parents (own) this building since 2000.

18. Andrew (break) his leg in Sunday night's game.
(He can't move his leg now.)

19. We (play) golf at the club since 1995.

20. They (marry) for nearly twenty years.

21. My husband (not smoke) a cigarette for three years now.

22. I'm excited because Charile Puth just (release) his new album.

23. We still (not decide) what to do this weekend.

24. My daughter (watch) the musical Lion King three times this week.

25. The house on the mountain (be) empty for eight years.

26. He (talk) on the phone for two hours.
(He is still talking on the phone.)

27. I (do) my assignment all afternoon.
(I am still doing my assignment.)

28. Sophia (work) too hard these last few weeks to finish up her dissertation.

29. I (read) the book I ordered online last month.

5

PAST PERFECT

5.1 Introduction

Past Perfect

Past perfect can refer to one past action that happened earlier than another past action. This aspect is only employed when the distinction in timing is necessary for our understanding of the relationship of the two actions. In addition, past perfect can indicate reported speech and unsatisfactory events in the past.

Past Perfect Progressive

Past perfect progressive can describe a continuing action that happened in the past, was still going on for some time in the past, and stopped at a certain moment in the past. This is usually used with a time-reference that indicates when the event began in the past and how long the event was in progress.

5.2 Usage

Past Perfect

1) Past perfect can represent permanent or long-lasting situations before another past event.

ex) The tree that had stood there for 100 years, fell in the storm yesterday.
She had joined the book club for a long time when she left.

2) Past perfect can express unrealized/unfulfilled wishes, intentions, and hopes.

ex) I had intended to go abroad, but I couldn't afford the money.
Kate had wanted to be an actress, but her boyfriend talked her out of it.

3) Past perfect can be used in a ***that-clause*** which is in the structures such as '*it was the first/second…that….*'

ex) It was the second time that I had been to China.
That was the first time Susan had talked to Mike.

4) Past perfect can be used in reported clauses that have the verbs such as *announce, mention, say, and tell.*

ex) Peter said he had already seen the film.
Someone told me that the restaurant had closed at 8 p.m.

5) Time conjunction such as ***after, as soon as, once*** and ***when*** can be used to talk about two events or activities that occurred one after the other. When past perfect is used with ***after, as soon as and so on***, the first event is not dependent of the second one and thus the two events are unrelated and separate; in other words, the first action ended before the second one began.

ex) When I had finished my assignment, my brother knocked on my door.
We didn't say anything as soon as he had started to talk.

Past Perfect Progressive

1) Past perfect progressive can be used to talk about temporary or short-term situations or activities before another past activity.

ex) My legs were painful because I had been waiting for 2 hours.
The girls had been making a cake for an hour when I arrived home.

2) Past perfect progressive can indicate the repetitive nature of a past event before another past action. When past perfect progressive can be used with a simple past, the past perfect progressive represents a longer background situation or activity; the simple past indicates a shorter event or activity that interrupted the longer situation or activity.

ex) John had been sleeping when his father called him up.
I had been living in New York when I met Nora.

Exercise

Put the verb into the correct form.

1. It was the first time that I (meet) a celebrity in my life.

2. He told me that his mother (be) sick for almost ten years.

3. I (watch) television when my husband got home.

4. As soon as I (finish) washing the dishes, I gave a call to Steve.

5. I (intend) to buy a cake, but I was busy cleaning the house.

6. She (live) in Japan for a few months before she moved to the United States.

7. I cleaned the house as soon as the plumber (go).

8. That was the first time I (catch) fish.

9. My grandparents (own) the garden for ten years before they handed it over to me.

10. After the company (fire) Linda, she tried to find a new job.

11. The movie already (start) when we arrived at the theater.

12. It was the third time my brother (hospitalize).

13. We (live) in Korea for fifteen years before we moved to America.

14. Thomas (be) sick for weeks before he finally visited a hospital.

15. We (hope) that Jack would be a dentist, but he wasn't good at science.

16. After I (finish) my work, I went out to have dinner.

17. It was the last time we (see) each other.

18. She bought a new car as soon as she (get) her driver's license.

19. I (drive) the car for three years before I sold it.

20. After we (eat) the seafood spaghetti, we had a bad stomach ache.

21. I (intend) to meet him, but I didn't have enough time.

22. She was tired because she (not sleep) well for several days.

23. Jonathan already (know) the news when I told him about it.

24. When I turned on the light, she already (leave) the room.

25. I (sit) for two hours, so my back began to hurt.

26. My brother (fix) his bicycle when I got home.

27. I gained weight after I (stop) exercising every day.

28. When the police arrested the robber, he already (spend) all the money.

29. We (talk) for an hour when Eric called me.

30. The property (belong) to me for years before Karen bought it.

6

FUTURE PERFECT

6.1 Introduction

Future Perfect

Future perfect can indicate activities that will continue or be finished by a specific future time.

Future Perfect Progressive

Future perfect progressive can state actions that still are in progress and will last for a certain period of time, but will be completed before a specific moment in the future.

6.2 Usage

Future Perfect

1) Future perfect can be used to talk about actions that will be completed before a certain moment in the future. (completion)

ex) We will have discussed several possible plans by tomorrow.
By the time Alex comes, I will have made a strawberry cake for him.

2) Future perfect can describe activities that will continue up until another activity in the future interrupt the previous activity. (ongoing)

ex) I will have prepared for the TOEFL Exam for a year by 2020.
James will have been in Paris for three months when we visit.

Future Perfect Progressive

Future perfect progressive can be used to talk about activities that currently continue and will last for a certain period of time, but will be finished before a specific moment in the future.

ex) Next month, I will have been teaching for 10 years.
By the time we arrive, Mike will have been preparing a dinner party for hours.

Exercise

Put the verb into the correct form.

1. We (know) each other for 10 years this July.

2. The baseball player (make) a contract by next week.

3. She (drive) for 3 hours by the time she gets home.

4. Sarah (take) a qualifying exam before she obtains her degree.

5. I (study) French for 5 years by the end of this year.

6. We (learn) a lot about English grammar by the end of this term.

7. His English (improve) enough to communicate before he moves to Australia.

8. I (be) in Berlin for 2 years by the time I leave.

9. We (complete) the report by this time tomorrow.

10. I (start) a new job before the end of this month.

11. The children (eat) their meal before you arrive.

12. Alex (receive) the letter by tomorrow.

13. By this time next year, my parents (marry) for forty years.

14. Sophia (receive) the scholarship when she enters the school in March.

15. By 2030, I hope researchers (discover) the cause of the incurable disease.

16. By the time Emma wakes up, I (prepare) dinner for her.

17. His ankle fully (heal) by next month.

18. I (save) enough money before I travel abroad.

19. By the time we travel to Mexico, we will (complete) the project.

20. Five days from now, I (finish) painting my house.

21. My brother (pay) off his loan by the time he gets married.

22. By the end of December, I (lose) 10kg by swimming.

23. I (help) my brother to do his assignment before the class starts.

24. At seven o'clock, we (wait) for fifty minutes.

25. In February, I (work) at the restaurant for five years.

26. By August, we (live) here for ten years.

27. My mother (teach) for 30 years when she retires.

7

AUXILIARY (MODAL) VERB

7.1 Introduction

Differences between Auxiliary and Modal Verbs

Auxiliary verbs are verbs which help the main verb to display its tense or to form questions or negation. Generally, there are four categories of auxiliary verb: have (has and had), be (is, was, and been), do (does and did), and will. In this sense, auxiliary verbs refer to grammatical or functional information such as *aspect, modality, mood, tense, and voice*. Meanwhile, modal verbs (can, could, may, might, must, ought to, shall, should, will, and would) are a category of auxiliary verbs that refer to the modality such as *ability, certainty, likelihood, obligation, or permission*. The key difference between auxiliary and modal verbs is that in general, auxiliary verbs are subject to change according to aspect, tense, and voice, while modal verbs do not change.

7.2 Usage

Degree of Certainty

The degree of certainty can be represented with ***will, must, should, may and might/could***. However, if something is true, a modal does not need to be used. For example, if someone says, "Mary is absent," he or she is sure; the degree of certainty is 100%.

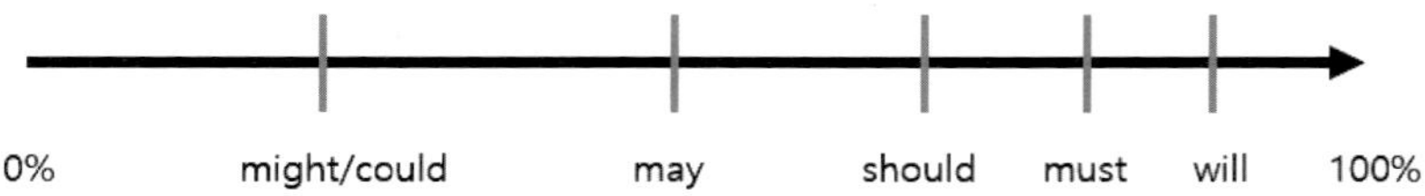

Will

Will can refer to a state of being certain or confident in the present or future. It can be used when somebody is sure that a circumstance is true or not true based on direct observation or shared knowledge.

ex) I'll be working on this essay all night.
Somebody is ringing the bell now. That will be Linda.

Must

Must can refer to the certainty that something is highly logical or reasonable. One believes that an event is quite logical if there is a plausible explanation for accepting it or for what is occurring.

ex) Look at all of that snow. It must be freezing outside.
She must live near here because she comes to school on foot.

Should

Should can represent what is probable or what is expected to emerge based on a logical expectation and assumption.

ex) They sent a parcel yesterday so it should arrive this week.
Jane should get home by now because I saw her off around 4p.m.

May

May can be used to show that something will possibly occur; there is a possibility of its happening.

ex) I think that may be a better solution.
We may go fishing at the lake this winter.

Might and Could

Might and could can indicate that something is probable in the future, but less certain.

ex) Maria usually goes shopping on Saturday mornings but she could be at home today.
I'm not sure where I put your phone away. It might be in the kitchen.

Degree of Obligation

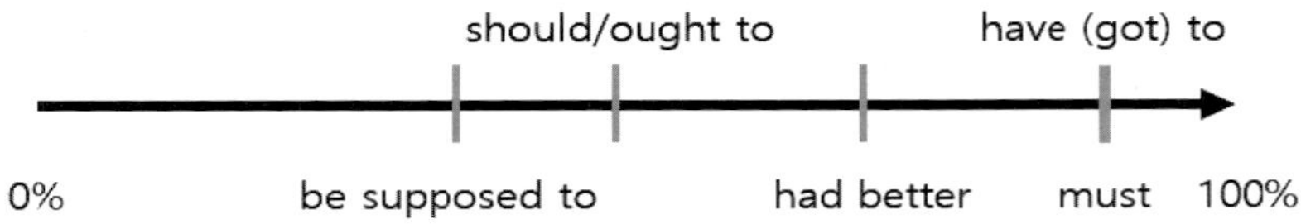

Must

Must can be used to say personal and subjective obligations. When ***must*** is used, the control and power for the obligations arises from the speaker.

ex) I really must stop smoking now.
You must wash your hands before eating food.

Have (got) To

In daily expressions of obligation, ***have (got) to*** is more frequently and commonly used than ***must***. In terms of degree of obligation, ***Have (got) to*** may be roughly equal to ***must.*** It displays an impersonal obligation. In other words, ***have (got) to*** indicates something that is socially necessary for us to do in a manner, and the obligation of ***have (got) to*** comes from outside such as *company's policies, laws, regulations, and social manners*.

ex) You have to keep quiet in the library.
We have got to wear a tie in our company.

Had Better

Had better can be used to talk about strong advice or order. ***Had better*** is quite similar to ***should and ought to,*** but it requires more urgent immediate action or attention and it is usually stronger than ***should and ought to***. If we do not follow the strong advice or order, we will get in trouble; there is no alternative or recommendable idea.

ex) You had better wake up now or you will be late.
My cold gets more serious. I had better see a doctor today.

Should and Ought to

Both ***should and ought to*** can be used to indicate duty and (moral) obligation. ***Should and ought to*** are quite similar and interchangeable. However, ***should*** is more frequently and commonly used than ***ought to.***

ex) You should never lie to your parents.
Your hair is too long. You ought to get a haircut.

Be Supposed To

Be supposed to can be used to express what someone is expected or required to do or is likely to do. ***Be supposed to*** can be sometimes replaced by ***be expected to*** but, may not be necessarily done. In addition, ***be supposed to*** can be employed for cultural expectations and rules.

ex) I'm supposed to feed my cat every day.
He was supposed to call you yesterday.
We are supposed to take off our shoes indoors in Korea.

Permission

Can and Could

Both ***can and could*** are used to ask and offer permission. ***Can*** is less formal and polite than ***could.***

ex) You can use my phone if you like.
Could I have some water, please?

May

May can be used to ask for or give permission in a formal way. It is used less frequently than ***can and could.***

ex) May I sit next to you?
You may go out when you finish your homework.

Will and Would

Will and would can refer to offers, promises, or requests in a polite and soft way. ***Will*** is less polite than ***would***.

ex) Would you like something to drink?
I will give you a ride home after the meeting.

Shall

Shall is the most commonly used in everyday English. In order to make suggestions and offers, it is in questions that ***shall*** is used the most frequently in everyday English: "Shall I ...?" or "Shall we ...?"

ex) Shall we dance?
It's hot. Shall I open the window?

Allow and Permit

Both ***allow and permit*** have very similar meanings of giving permission, but ***permit*** is more formal. ***A direct object + to infinitive*** can follow after ***allow*** and ***permit***. In addition, instead of ***allow***, ***permit*** is only employed in a passive sentence where ***it*** is used as a subject.

ex) Smoking is not permitted/allowed in this building.
It is not permitted to smoke in this building.
It is not allowed to smoke. (x)
My parents allowed me to go to the party.

Ability

Can and Could

Can and could represents an idea about general, physical or mental ability; someone or something is able to do something and knows the way to do something. ***Could*** is employed to express the ability in the past.

ex) Cats can see in the dark.
I can translate from English to Korean.
I could read before I entered school.
When Tom was young, he could speak several languages.

Be Able To

Be able to can be used to talk about abilities and it can refer to a single event or a particular occasion of success. In addition, ***can*** is not placed after another modal verb, but ***be able to*** can be placed.

ex) We were able to get to the meeting on time.
The lawyer will be able to see you next Monday.

7.3 Can/Could vs. Be Able To

Can/Could represents general abilities; something can be done at any time in the past or in the present. However, ***be able to*** represents abilities with a singular completion or specific success.

ex) I practiced driving during the summer. By winter, I **could** drive well. (multiple events or ongoing activity)
I practiced driving during the summer. By winter, I **was able to** pass my driving test. (single event)

7.4 Would vs. Used to vs. Simple Past

Something that occurred in the past but does not take place anymore can be expressed in different ways. ***Used to*** is employed for past actions and states that don't occur now. ***Would*** can be used to express repeated past actions. Consequently, the major difference between ***used to*** and ***would*** is that ***used to*** can be employed with action verbs as well as stative verbs, while ***would*** is only employed with action verbs. Like ***used to, simple past*** is used to represent repeated past action or past states. However, when something took place only once, ***the simple past*** must be used instead of ***used to or would.***

	Would	Used to	Simple Past
Repetitive Past Action	○	○	○
Repetitive Past State	×	○	○
Single Occurrence	×	×	○

ex) I **went/would/used to** go swimming every summer. (repetitive past action)

I **used to have/had** a cat called Diana. (repetitive past state)

I **went** to Canada in 2000. (occurred only once in the past)

7.5 Will vs. Should

Will can describe predicted or scheduled events. It can describe what is scheduled or predicted to happen with more certainty based on information, time table, or computation. Meanwhile, ***should*** can represent what we logically expect with less certainty based on personal insights, inference, or intuition.

ex) Tom **will** visit us on Saturday.
(Tom is scheduled to visit us.)
Tom **should** visit us on Saturday. (Based on my insight, Tom is logically expected to visit us.)

7.6 Must vs. Have To

Both ***must*** and ***have to*** can state one's duty or responsibility. However, ***must*** can express duties or responsibilities which come from the speaker's judgement. ***Have to*** can indicate duties or responsibilities which come from outside such as *laws, regulations, and someone's orders*.

ex) I **must** stop smoking. (I need to stop smoking.)
I **have to** stop smoking.
(The doctor has strongly advised me to stop smoking.)

7.7 Should Have P.P vs. Would Have P.P

Based on personal insight, inference, intuition with less certainty, ***should have p.p*** can refer to a past expectation with disappointment which was not realized. Unlike ***should have p.p,*** based on information, schedule, or calculation with more certainty, ***would have p.p*** can represent an unsuccessful/unfulfilled effort; ***would have p.p*** can be used for something that was scheduled to occur but did not occur. ***Would have p.p*** often precedes a reason.

ex) His album **should have been released** last week.
(His album was expected to be released with less certainty, but it wasn't released. It makes me disappointed now.)
His album **would have been released** last week.
(His album was scheduled (=predicted) to be released with more certainty, but it wasn't released for situational reasons such as *a company bankruptcy*.)

* ***Expect*** is to anticipate or look forward to the coming or occurrence of something on the basis of personal insight and inference. On the other hand, ***predict*** is to foretell or declare in advance based on observation, knowledge, or scientific reason. Meanwhile, ***schedule*** is to plan that something will happen at a particular time such as *time-tabled activities*.

7.8 Should Have P.P vs. Could Have P.P

Should have p.p can express an opinion or advice for a past event and it can be used to talk about past mistakes and disappointment. Unlike ***should have p.p, Could have p.p*** can refer to a suggestion for a past option not selected. Namely, someone had the capability to do something, but did not try to do it.

ex) I **should have entered** Harvard University. (It could be better for me to enter Harvard University but the idea was not realized.)

I **could have entered** Harvard university, but I entered University of Maryland at College Park (UMCP) instead. (It was possible for me to enter Harvard University, but I made a choice to enter UMCP.)

7.9 Could Have P.P vs. Might Have P.P

Could have p.p can be used for unfulfilled past abilities or missed opportunities. In other words, someone was able to achieve something in the past, but did not make an attempt to do it; or something was feasible in the past, but did not occur. Unlike this, ***might have p.p*** can present the possibility that something was true or occurred in the past.

ex) He **could have left** the party earlier. (He was able to leave the party earlier but did not try to leave.)

He **might have left** the party earlier. (It is possible/true that he left the party earlier but we are not sure whether he left or not.)

Exercise

A. Decide if these sentences denote Certainty (C), Obligation (O), Permission (P) or Ability (A).

1. It **should** be raining now, according to the weather forecast.

2. **May** I ask a question please?

3. You **must** do your homework before dinner.

4. Tomas **could** answer the phone but he is usually busy working at this time of the day.

5. All employees **have to** attend a meeting every Monday mornings.

6. **Would** you mind if I open the window?

7. Jay **could** run very fast when he was younger.

8. You haven't eaten all day. You **must** be hungry.

9. I **had better** go now before I am faced with a traffic jam.

10. Jane **may** be at home, or perhaps at work.

11. You **can** go home now if you want to.

12. You **should** brush your teeth after every meal.

13. Financial experts **can** help you make decisions with your money.

14. I think we **will** be late for the appointment.

15. Helen **ought to** exercise more to lose weight.

16. It **is not permitted to** swim in this river.

17. I'**m supposed to** walk my dog every weekend.

18. I **was able to** submit my application earlier than the due date.

19. **May** I borrow your cell phone to call my sister?

20. As she is a veterinarian, she **must** know a lot about animals.

B. Select the correct answers to complete the following sentences.

1. It's a secret. You ________ tell anyone what I just told you.

   a. might not
   b. must not
   c. may not
   d. will not

2. I'm not sure, but she ________ come to the party tomorrow.

   a. will
   b. must
   c. might/may
   d. should

3. My car will not start at all. There _________ be something wrong with the engine of the car.

   a. might
   b. shall
   c. used to
   d. must

4. ________ you help me with my luggage, please?

a. May
b. Could
c. Might
d. Shall

5. She is pretty busy these days, but she ________ be able to see you next week.

a. should
b. can
c. must
d. may

6. We ________ get to the airport by three or else we could miss the flight.

a. might
b. will
c. had better
d. may

7. As Maria has travelled a lot, she ________ speak many languages.

a. can
b. may

c. might

d. would

8. When she was a teenager, she _______ sleep late on Sundays.

a. will

b. would

c. might

d. could

9. Peter ________ quit his job because he is moving to another country.

a. would

b. may

c. must

d. might

10. Don't worry about her. I'm sure she ________ feel better soon.

a. could

b. may

c. might

d. will

C. Identify the answers of the sentences below.

1. I'm really tired today. I (should have gone / would have gone) to the bed earlier last night.

2. I could not see her face, but I thought she (might have smiled / could have smiled).

3. He (should have been / could have been) a doctor but he decided to become a lawyer instead.

4. As the exam was difficult, only a few students (could / were able to) pass it.

5. By law, each person in the vehicle (has to / must) wear a seat belt.

6. There (used to be / would be / was) a coffeehouse on that corner.

7. My family (used to go / would go / went) camping often when I was young.

8. My friend (used to fly / would fly / flew) to Roma via Napoli a week ago.

8

Passive

8.1 Introduction

There are two types of voices, which express the relationship between the subject and the action: active and passive. If an actor or agent occupies the subject of a sentence, one can use an active structure (i.e., catch, tell, and write). On the other hand, if the recipient or patient that undergoes the action occupies the subject of a sentence, one can use a passive structure (i.e., is caught, was told, and are written). In general, the object of an active structure is identical to the subject of a passive structure. When a passive structure is used, the subject of the active verb can be optionally used in a ***by***-phrase.

8.2 Usage

1) Passive voice can be formed by using the auxiliary ***be*** + the past participle of the verb.

ex) My phone was fixed yesterday.
The document is being sent right now.
A bridge is going to be built within the next three months.

2) Intransitive verbs (i.e., appear, arrive, consist of, happen, and occur) cannot be acceptable in the passive voice because these verbs do not have objects in the active voice. Meanwhile, some transitive verbs, especially stative verbs such as ***fit, have*** and, ***resemble***, which refer to states, are less commonly used in the passive voice.

ex) My favorite singer appeared on TV. (o)
My favorite singer was appeared on TV. (x)
We have a big garden. (o)
A big garden is had by us. (x)
The girl resembles her mother. (o)
Her mother is resembled by the girl. (x)

3) Dative (ditransitive) verbs (i.e., give, lend, offer, promise, send, show, teach, and tell) have both an indirect object (I.O) and a direct object (D.O) in a sentence.

3-1) In some cases, the I.O can be placed immediately after the D.O with a preposition such as ***to*** and ***for***. In the passive voice, either an I.O or a D.O can be used as the subject of the sentence. However, be cautious that only the I.O can often become the subject of passive verb in the type of I.O D.O. In addition, the I.O cannot become the subject of a passive verb in the type of only D.O to I.O.

3-2) Type of Dative Verb

To	bring, give, hand, offer, pass, send, show, teach, tell etc.
For	bake, build, buy, cook, do, get, make, order, prepare etc.
Only I.O D.O	allow, cost, deny, envy, forgive, guarantee, permit, refuse etc.
Only D.O to I.O	announce, explain, introduce, mention, prove, report, suggest etc.

3-3) When a D.O is used as the subject of the passive sentence, a preposition such as ***to*** or ***for*** is followed by the indirect object.

ex) Nobody can bring you peace but yourself.
My husband gave the beautiful flowers to me.
My mother always makes the various dishes for our family.
The government refused him a visa.

The chairman announced the plan to us.

You can be brought peace by nobody but yourself.

Peace can be brought to you by nobody but yourself.

The beautiful flowers were given to me by my husband.

I was given the beautiful flowers by my husband.

The various dishes are always made for our family by my mother.

He was refused a visa (by the office). (o)

A visa was refused him (by the office). (x)

The plan was announced to us (by the chairman). (o)

We were announced the plan (by the chairman). (x)

4) When it comes to phrasal verbs ***[verb + adverb (i.e., bring up, hold back, and take up)]*** and prepositional verbs ***[verb + (adverb) + preposition (i.e., catch up with, depend on, do away with, and put up with)]***, the verbs should be followed by their participles in the passive structure. The adverb and the preposition cannot be omitted.

ex) The baby is taken care of by the nurse.

The meeting was put off by my boss.

5) If a sentence has an object clause, the passive structure can often be possible with a grammatical (dummy) subject, ***it*** as the subject of the sentence.

ex) People say that money is not the key to happiness.
That money is not the key to happiness is said by people. (x)
It is said that money is not the key to happiness.
Money is said not to be the key to happiness.

6) Some verbs (i.e., advise, ask, force, request, tell, and want) can precede ***object*** + ***infinitive***. In the case of these verbs, the passive structure can be possible: ***Object*** + ***Be*** + ***P.P*** + ***To-infinitive.*** Meanwhile, the causative verbs (i.e., help, let, and make) and the perceptive verbs (i.e., feel, hear, listen, notice, observe, see, and watch) precede ***object*** + ***a bare infinitive*** (the base form of the verb without ***to***) in active structures, but ***to-infinitives*** are followed in passive structures. When a perceptive verb is placed in a passive structure, ***v***-ing (present participle) can be used instead of the bare infinitive in order to describe that an action is still ongoing for a while.

ex) The patient is advised to eat more vegetables.
She is asked to send a package.
I was helped to find a jacket in my size by the clerk.
He is made to prepare for the presentation.
The woman was seen crossing/to cross the street yesterday.

Exercise

Sentences are given in the active voice. Change them into the passive voice.

1. The Wright brothers invented the airplane.

   The airplane ____________ by the Wright brothers.

   a. was invented

   b. is invented

   c. is being invented

2. We saw him stand in front of the department store.

   He ____________ in front of the department store (by us).

   a. was seen stand

   b. saw to stand

   c. was seen to stand

3. My brother has not cleaned the room yet.

   The room ____________ by my brother yet.

   a. hasn't been cleaned

   b. hasn't cleaning

   c. hasn't had cleaned

4. The doctor told me to quit smoking immediately.
   I ____________ smoking immediately by the doctor.

   a. told to quit
   b. was told to quit
   c. was told quit

5. People think that health is the most important thing.
   Health is thought ________ the most important thing.

   a. to have been
   b. that
   c. to be

6. They asked John to make a speech at the meeting.
   John ____________ a speech at the meeting (by them).

   a. was asked to make
   b. was asked make
   c. was ask to make

7. My sister is going to look after my dog during the holidays.
   My dog ____________ during the holidays (by my sister).

   a. is going to looked after
   b. is going to be looked after
   c. is going to be looked

8. The manager offered him several jobs.

He ____________ several job by the manager.

a. was offered

b. was offered to

c. was being offered

9. A bus ran over the man yesterday.

The man ____________ by a bus yesterday.

a. was ran

b. was run over

c. run over

10. They gave me a fine for parking my car in the wrong place.

I ____________ a fine for parking my car in the wrong place.

a. was given

b. was given to

c. was given for

11. His mother bought him a laptop computer.

A laptop computer ____________ him (by his mother).

a. was bought

b. was bought to

c. was bought for

12. I'm not going to put up with his smoking any longer.

His smoking ____________ any longer.

a. isn't going to be put up

b. isn't going to put up with

c. isn't going to be put up with

13. The teacher saw the students walking out of the school.

The students ____________ out of the school (by the teacher).

a. were seen to walk

b. were seen walking

c. were seen to walking

14. My customer sent me several complaint letters.

Several complaint letters ____________ me (by my customer).

a. were sent to

b. were sent for

c. were sent by

15. Everyone has spoken highly of this movie.

This movie ____________ by everyone.

a. has spoke highly of

b. has been spoken highly

c. has been spoken highly of

16. My girlfriend brought me a sandwich for lunch.

A sandwich ___________ for lunch (by my girlfriend).

a. was brought to me

b. brought to me

c. was brought for me

17. The teacher explained English grammar to his students.

English grammar ___________ his students (by the teacher).

a. was explained for

b. is explained to

c. was explained to

18. People envy Daniel his energy and passion in the life.

Daniel ___________ his energy and passion in the life.

a. is envied

b. envied by

c. is envied to

9

DETERMINER AND NOUN

9.1 Introduction

Determiner

Determiners (i.e., articles: *a, an, the*; demonstratives: *this, that*; possessives: *his or whose*; quantifiers: *any, either, some, few, little*) make the meaning (=denotation) of a noun phrase (NP) specific. There are some shared grammatical similarities among all determiners. Determiners are located at the beginning of a NP and more than one determiner cannot be usually used in the same NP; if more than one determiner are used, those are typically used in a certain order [i.e., a friend of mine (double possessive)].

Noun

Nouns are words that indicate a person, animal, thing, or place and these serve as the subject, object, and complement of a sentence. In addition, nouns can be connected with determiners and be classified as singular or plural.

9.2 Usage

Determiner

1) Articles such as ***'a(n)' and 'the'*** are types of determiners. ***'A(n)'*** is called an indefinite article and ***'the'*** is called a definite article. ***'A(n)'*** and ***'the'*** can also represent the specificity and definiteness of a noun.

1-1) ***A(n)*** can be placed before singular nouns when the listener/reader cannot exactly identify something that they are talking about.

ex) She has finally got a good job.
My brother lives in a small town.

On top of that, ***a(n)*** can be used when one member of a class is typical of the whole class.

ex) A cello is an important part of an orchestra.
A doctor must be present at each athletic contest.

1-2) ***The*** can be placed before a noun (i.e., countable: singular or plural; uncountable) when referring to something that has been mentioned before or the listener/speaker can clearly identify from the situation that they are talking about.

ex) I bought a bag yesterday. The bag is big enough for all my luggage.
The girl sitting next to me raised her hands.
Could you close the window?

In addition, ***the*** can be used to indicate something that is only one in the universe or in the context (e.g., the government, the sun, and the universe). For the same reason, ***the*** can be used with superlatives.

ex) The Earth revolves around the sun.
The government has increased taxes again this year.
Peter is the tallest student in the class.
Mona Lisa is the most expensive painting in the world.

1-3) ***No article (zero article)*** can be used when talking or writing about something in general and not referring to a specific object. An uncountable noun is used with no article (e.g., milk, rice, and water). A countable noun is used with -(e)s, the plural form (e.g., apartments, cars, and cats).

ex) Life is valuable.
Dolphins are known for their friendliness.
This shirt is made of pure cotton.
My father bought red roses for me.

1-4) To talk about a general thing, not only ***a(an)*** but also ***plural countable nouns without an article*** can be used. In addition, ***the*** sometimes can express generality with a singular countable noun. Generic ***the*** is usually used with:

(a) species of animals: The tiger is found only in Asia.
(b) inventions: Who invented the radio?
(c) instruments: Can you play the violin?

ex) He needs a straw for this orange juice.
Cats are more independent and intelligent than dogs.
The red rose stands for love and passion.

The definitions of definiteness and specificity are given below.

Definitions of Definiteness and Specificity

If a Determiner Phrases (DP) of the form [D NP] is

a. [+definite], then the speaker and hearer presuppose the existence of a unique individual in the set denoted by the NP.
b. [+specific], then the speaker intends to refer to a unique individual in the set denoted by the NP and considers this individual to possess some noteworthy property. (Ionin, Ko, & Wexler, 2004, p. 5)

Predictions for Article Choice in L2-English

	[+definite] target: the	[-definite] target: a
+ specific	correct use of **the**	overuse of **the**
- specific	overuse of **a**	correct use of **a**

(Ionin et al., 2004, p. 19)

(a) [+definite, +specific]

Kathy: My daughter Jeannie loves that new comic strip about Super Mouse.

Elise: Well, she is in luck! Tomorrow, I'm having lunch with (a / the / no article) creator of this comic strip—-he is an old friend of mine. So I can get his autograph for Jeannie!

(b) [+definite, - specific]

At a gallery

Sarah: Do you see that beautiful landscape painting?

Mary: Yes, it's wonderful.

Sarah: I would like to meet (an / the / no article) author of that painting; unfortunately, I have no idea who it is, since the painting is not signed.

(c) [- definite, +specific]

In a "Lost and Found"

Clerk: Can I help you? Are you looking for something you lost?

Customer: Yes . . . I realize you have a lot of things here, but maybe you have what I need. You see, I am looking for (a / the / no article) green scarf. I think that I lost it here last week.

(d) [- definite, -specific]

In a school

Student: I am new in this school. This is my first day.

Teacher: Welcome! Are you going to be at the school party tonight?

Student: Yes. I'd like to get to know my classmates. I am hoping to find (a / the / no article) new good friend! I don't like being all alone.

(The conversations above were adapted from Ionin et al., 2004, pp. 65-67)

2) Demonstratives such as *this/these and that/those* indicate something that is close to or distant from the speaker or writer.

ex) Look at that bright star.

He doesn't want to see this movie.

3) Possessives (i.e., her, his, its, my, our, their, and your) prior to nouns refer to ownership of the nouns.

ex) Jack sold his house last month.

My aunt will visit me this Saturday.

4) Quantifiers (i.e., all, few, little, many, and much) represent how much or many of something is being expressed in a noun phrase.

ex) Please give me every flower you have.
Few of the students wanted to study Physics.

5) The cardinal numbers (i.e., one, two, three) and ordinal numbers (i.e., first, second, third) are one type of determiners.

ex) Kate ordered two cakes.
I went to France for the second time this year.

Noun

1) Countable Nouns vs. Uncountable Nouns
Noun can be either countable or uncountable.

1-1) Countable nouns are something that can be counted; they have both singular and plural forms. In the singular, it can be paired with the determiner '***a(n)***' or '***the***'; in the plural, '***(e)s***' is added to the end.

1-2) Uncountable nouns, also called as mass nouns (i.e., music, art, love, advice, information, news, furniture, luggage, rice, sugar, butter, water, electricity, gas, power, money, and currency etc.) are something that cannot be counted with numbers; they are abstract ideas, substance, and concepts that cannot be split into discrete elements. Uncountable nouns are usually paired with a singular verb.

One can use an expression like some, any, much, a little, a lot of, a great deal of (i.e., a little/some money, much/any rice) or a unit of measurement like quantity + measurement unit + uncountable noun (i.e., two slices of bread, five items of clothing, a piece of news, three bottles of water) in order to count an uncountable noun or specify a quantity of an uncountable noun.

ex) My brother bought a laptop last month.
I would like three pens, please.
This news is very urgent.
Her luggage looks heavy.
He gave me a good deal of advice before my interview.
We'll get a discount if we buy three or more items of clothing.

2) Common Nouns Vs. Proper Nouns

Common nouns are general names that refer to a class of objects such as *areas, buildings, countries, organizations, parks, people, planets*. They can be singular (chair) or plural (chairs); countable (desk) or uncountable (information); concrete (pencil) or abstract (love). In contrast with common nouns, proper nouns are the unique names of a person, thing, or place and they always begin with a capital letter.

ex) I like looking at old bridges.

Barack Obama served as the 44th president of the United States.

3) Concrete nouns are nouns that point to people or things, which can be physically touched, smelled, tasted, heard, or seen (i.e., apple, building, dog, and tree). However, abstract nouns are nouns that point to intangible things such as *concepts, states, qualities, ideas, conditions, and emotions*, which cannot be physically touched, smelled, tasted, heard, or seen (i.e., friendship, happiness, humor, love and truth).

ex) Please remember to buy apples.

Sometimes it takes courage to tell the truth.

4) Collective nouns point out groups or units which consist of more than one person or thing (i.e., audience, family, government, jury, and team). They can take either a singular or plural form, depending on how one treats the individuals or members in a group; if the individuals of a group are performing collectively as a whole or one single unit (entity), one treats them as singular or if the members of a group are performing individually, one treats them as plural.

ex) The jury has made its decision, based on only the facts presented.

(The individuals in the jury are acting together as a whole.)

The jury have not made a decision because they are still arguing one another.
(The members in the jury are acting individually.)

5) Compound nouns are noun phrases made up of two or more words. Most compound nouns are composed of nouns modified by adjectives (adjective + noun: blackboard) or other nouns (noun + noun: football). They are occasionally one word (i.e., bedroom, haircut, and toothpaste). In addition, those can be connected with a hyphen (i.e., dry-cleaning, one-stop, and well-being). Sometimes, compound nouns are two separate words (i.e., Christmas tree, full moon, and swimming pool).

ex) Is this the bus stop for the number 26 bus?
The student is writing on the blackboard.

Exercise

A. Choose one out of the three articles a(n), the, or no article in parentheses (round brackets).

(a) Context 1

Two students are talking about the articles presented in the class.

Student 1 : Did you get any research paper on psycholinguistics?

Student 2 : I got a research paper. I think that ***(an/the/no article)*** article will be a good one. I think that the professor will like it.

(b) Context 2

A conversation between two people about the possibility of climbing Mount Everest by an old man.

Bill : It is really impossible for an old man to climb Mount Everest. How do you think?

Henry : I can't agree with this. Nothing is impossible in human life. I am trying to find ***(an/the/no article)*** old man who is in training to climb Mount Everest. I will get all information about him very shortly.

(c) Context 3

Two friends are talking to each other after shopping.

Friend 1 : Let's go back to dormitory. You have already bought several items of clothing.

Friend 2 : Yes, I bought many things. I also need ***(a/the/no article)*** school bag like one my friend bought two days ago.

(d) Context 4

Conversation between two foreign students

Student 1 : I'm facing some academic difficulties. So I am trying to meet ***(an/the/no article)*** academic advisor. I think it would help me out. But I am new to this university. How can I meet with him?

Student 2 : Although it is a little bit late, that is a right decision. You can get his e-mail ID from the website of our university.

(The conversations above were adapted from Sarker & Baek, 2017, p. 375)

B. Choose the correct answer.

1. He got his license without _______ problems.

   a. some
   b. any
   c. every
   d. each

2. _______ cupcakes are so tasty. Can I have another?

a. That
b. This
c. Here
d. These

3. This is the _______ time I have ever eaten lamb.

a. first
b. some
c. one
d. any

4. My aunt takes _______ dog for a walk in the morning.

a. she
b. hers
c. her
d. herself

5. There aren't _______ students in the library.

a. much
b. many
c. every
d. little

6. Could you bring me _______ flowers I left on the table?

a. here
b. this
c. that
d. those

7. She was wearing a bracelet on _______ wrist.

a. all
b. each
c. any
d. some

8. _______ grandfather used to take us fishing.

a. Our
b. We
c. Ourselves
d. Ours

9. Unfortunately, I have _______ talent for art although I have always wanted to be a famous artist.

a. many
b. a few
c. few
d. little

10. She always keeps _______ money for emergencies.

a. all
b. some
c. any
d. every

C. Choose the correct types of the nouns for the underlined words.

1. Drinking **water** can lower blood pressure.

a. Countable
b. Proper
c. Collective
d. Uncountable

2. How many **classrooms** are there in your school?

a. Compound
b. Proper
c. Abstract
d. Uncountable

3. **Cats** show their affection in ways very different from other pets.

a. Abstract

b. Common

c. Proper

d. Compound

4. The children are flying **kites** on the hill.

a. Uncountable

b. Compound

c. Proper

d. Countable

5. The whole **family** should wait to see the doctor at the table.

a. Proper

b. Collective

c. Compound

d. Abstract

6. There was an earthquake in **Indonesia** on Tuesday.

a. Proper

b. Common

c. Compound

d. Abstract

7. **Education** is the most powerful weapon to change the world.

a. Concrete
b. Abstract
c. Common
d. Countable

8. People are already eating more **salt** than they need.

a. Countable
b. Compound
c. Concrete
d. Abstract

9. Our **team** played really well today.

a. Abstract
b. Compound
c. Proper
d. Collective

10. I've bought a new **dress** for spring.

a. Proper
b. Countable
c. Collective
d. Abstract

11. It was **Edison** who invented the phonograph.

a. Abstract
b. Proper
c. Common
d. Compound

12. In 1947, India got its **freedom** to be a sovereign country.

a. Proper
b. Concrete
c. Collective
d. Abstract

13. **Toothpaste** now comes in many flavors.

a. Compound
b. Collective
c. Abstract
d. Proper

14. She teaches **music** at a public high school.

a. Abstract
b. Countable
c. Compound
d. Concrete

15. We bought some **tomatoes** in the market.

a. Proper
b. Collective
c. Countable
d. Abstract

16. I used to play outside with my friends during my **childhood**.

a. Countable
b. Concrete
c. Proper
d. Abstract

17. **Neil Armstrong** landed on the moon in 1969.

a. Abstract
b. Proper
c. Collective
d. Common

18. My mother's **health** is the only problem to me.

a. Countable
b. Compound
c. Concrete
d. Abstract

10
PRONOUN

10.1 Introduction

Pronouns can be used as replacements for nouns or noun phrases which have already been mentioned or whose referents are already known in order to avoid repetition of the nouns or noun phrases.

10.2 Usage

1) Subject pronouns can be used in place of nouns which are the subject of their clauses in order to avoid repeating the subject.

ex) He doesn't like pancakes.
This chair is broken. It needs to be repaired.

2) Object pronouns can be used as substitutes for nouns that are either the indirect or direct object of a verb, or are the object of a preposition.

ex) Give the pencil to me.
Jane invited him to dinner on Sunday night.
My mother taught me English.
I've been waiting for her since 1 pm.

3) Possessive pronouns can refer to a type of pronoun that replaces something possessed by either someone or something (i.e., animal or thing), which is previously mentioned.

ex) That was not my mistake. It was yours.
I found my bag but Maria could not find hers.

4) Demonstrative pronouns can refer to something which is nearby (i.e., this, these) or far away (i.e., that, those) in space or time.

ex) This is my present for you.
That looks like a small cat.
That is a brilliant idea.
These are beautiful flowers but smell bad.

5) Indefinite pronouns (i.e., all, any, each, every, few, and some) can represent one or more unspecified beings, places, or objects.

ex) Everyone says he is polite.
Somebody ate my hamburger!

6) Interrogative pronouns (i.e., who, whom, whose, which, and what) can be used in order to ask questions. In other words, they are employed to ask a specific question or an indirect question. ***Who, whom, and whose*** point only to people, but other interrogative pronouns can indicate people or objects. In some cases, interrogative pronouns can take on suffix "-ever" (i.e., whoever, whomever, whichever, and whatever).

ex) He asked which subway to take.
What do you want for lunch?
You can invite whomever you like.
Choose whichever you want.
Whose cell phone is this?
I'll do whatever I can to help you.

7) Reflexive pronouns can be employed when the subject and object are the same. The reflexive pronouns refer back to the subject and object of the sentence, and possessives.

ex) ***Students*** should improve ***themselves*** in every possible way.
We will devote ***ourselves*** to something that makes our life better and more valuable.
All ***her*** money was spent on clothes for ***herself***.
I am going to tell ***him*** a bit of gossip about ***himself***.

7-1) A personal pronoun such as *you and me* can be followed after a preposition of place when the meaning is clear without a reflexive pronoun.

ex) ***She*** looked at ***her/herself*** in the mirror every day.
He was pulling a small wheelbarrow behind ***him***.

7-2) Reflexives can be used for emphasis on the person or thing which is previously mentioned.

ex) ***You*** can do it ***yourself***.
He's brought ***himself*** something to eat.

7-3) Reflexives can replace personal pronouns after ***as, but(for), and except (for).***

ex) Everybody laughed loudly ***except*** me/myself.

7-4) There is a difference in meaning between -***selves*** and **each other/one another.**

ex) They (Tom and David) talk to themselves every day.
(= Each of them speaks to himself; Each person engages in self-talk; Tom talks to Tom; David talks to David.)
They talk to each other every day.
(= One of them talks to the other; Tom talks to David; David talks to Tom.)

8) Relative pronouns are pronouns that introduce a relative clause and these pronouns can be usually used to join two sentences (See Ch.15)

ex) The car which Tom drives is very expensive.
I am looking for someone who can take care of my baby.

Exercise

Choose the correct answer.

1. I talked to the woman _______ car had parked in front of the restaurant.

   a. which
   b. who
   c. whose
   d. her

2. My daughter Sarah loves books. This novel is for _______ .

   a. she
   b. her
   c. hers
   d. herself

3. The boy looked at _______ in the mirror.

   a. his
   b. him
   c. he
   d. himself

4. The boy looks at _______ in the mirror every morning.

a. his
b. him
c. he
d. himself

5. We traveled around Europe for 3 weeks. _______ was an interesting experience.

a. Those
b. They
c. These
d. That

6. _______ do you think will win the playoff game?

a. How
b. When
c. Who
d. Why

7. John and Carol haven't met _______ for a long time.

a. them
b. they
c. each other
d. theirs

8. I feel tired this evening. I've been working hard _______ .

a. each day
b. all day
c. someday
d. any day

9. You'll have to get your own pen. _______ is mine.

a. These
b. This
c. They
d. Those

10. I didn't repair the car _______. Someone else did it for me.

a. me
b. myself
c. mine
d. my

11. We met Kevin and Nancy yesterday. This house is _______ .

a. theirs
b. their
c. they
d. them

12. My grandparents live in Seoul. _______ visit us often.

a. Their
b. Them
c. They
d. Themselves

13. Alex called several times but _______ answered.

a. somebody
b. anybody
c. nobody
d. everybody

14. _______ wants to go to the movies with me?

a. Who
b. What
c. Which
d. Whose

15. Maria likes to do thing by ________ .

a. myself
b. her
c. yourself
d. herself

16. _______ spent more time walking a century ago.

a. Some person
b. Each people
c. All person
d. All people

17. The shirt _______ I bought yesterday is already stained.

a. what
b. who
c. which
d. it

18. The two boys threw the ball back and forth to _______ .

a. each other
b. their
c. them
d. theirs

19. _______ would you prefer, coffee or tea?

a. Why
b. Who
c. What
d. Which

20. Indian mangoes are better than _______ of Thailand.

a. those
b. these
c. that
d. this

21. ________ do you want to get on your birthday?

a. How
b. Why
c. Who
d. What

11
SUBJECT-VERB AGREEMENT

11.1 Introduction

The verb of a sentence is determined by the subject of the sentence on the basis of number (singular or plural) and person [the first person (I and we), second person (you) or third person (he, she, they, it and nouns)].

11.2 Usage

1) When the subjects are linked by 'and,' the verb takes plural, but in the case that the compound subjects represent a singular idea, the verb takes singular. Besides, when the two singular subjects are linked by 'or,' the verb takes singular.

ex) Harry or Sally works at the Marketing department.
My father and mother prepare dinner together every weekend.
Bread and butter is my favourite breakfast.

2) Proximity agreement is the rule of depending on the noun that is closest to the verb to determine whether the verb takes singular or plural. This rule applies to the subjects including the following expressions: *either X or Y*, *neither X nor Y*, *not only X but also Y*, *X or Y*, *X together with Y*, and *X as well as Y*.

ex) Neither Jack nor his brothers play basketball.
Is either the teacher or the students going to clean the boards?

3) Collective nouns such as *staff, committee and team* can be either singular or plural. Collective nouns take singular verb form when one regards the group as a single unit (entity); however, these take plural verb form when one regards the group as individual members or separate things acting within the whole.

ex) Our staff does some voluntary work on Saturday mornings.
Our staff work hard to achieve their goals.
A dozen eggs is probably not enough to feed the entire group.
Mr. Johnson ordered five hen eggs and seven duck eggs. The one dozen eggs were delivered to him this morning.
Only half a dozen (people) are coming over to the party this afternoon.

4) When pronoun subjects such as *'all' 'half,' 'some,' 'more,' or 'none,'* are followed by a prepositional phrase, the object of the preposition determines whether the verb takes singular or plural.

ex) Half of the population is in favour of reform.
Fifty percent of the students want to become teachers.

5) The words ***here*** and ***there*** have generally been labeled as an adverb even though they refer to place. In sentences beginning with ***here*** or ***there***, which functions as a grammatical or dummy subject, the verb follows the real subject.

ex) There is a flower on the table.
There are some flowers on the table.

6) Expressions of distance, measurement, money, and time take singular verbs when the amount is regarded as one single unit; otherwise, those can take a plural verb, when the amount is considered as individual segments or units.

ex) Ten minutes were left for countdown.
Two years is a long time to be without a job

7) Exceptionally, some nouns (i.e., customs, mathematics, news, and savings) are always plural, but they take singular verbs because they actually refer to one single unit (entity) composed of smaller and uncountable parts.

ex) Mathematics is not my favorite subject.
The news was broadcasted last evening.

8) The expression 'the number' is followed by a singular verb while the expression 'a number' is followed by a plural verb.

ex) A large number of traffic accidents occur every year.
The total number of refugees has continued to rise.

9) A noun *'clothes'* only takes a plural verb and the word *'clothes'* refers to the things that people wear to cover their bodies. Meanwhile, the word *'clothe'* is not a singular noun form of *'clothes,'* but a verb form which refers to putting clothes on someone or providing clothes for someone. In addition, the plural noun *'clothes'* should be distinguished from a singular *'a cloth'* or plural noun *'cloths'* which means a piece of fabric. Finally, an uncountable noun *'clothing'* refers to a particular type of clothes such as *sports clothing, winter clothing or waterproof clothing*. When specifying a particular number of clothing, *'an item (article/piece) of clothing'* or *'two items (articles/pieces) of clothing'* can be used.

ex) Her new clothes look great.

Parents tend to clothe their children in the latest fashions.

The jacket is made from woolen cloths.

You'll get a discount if you buy three or more items of clothing

They are desperate to collect food and clothing for the poor.

10) The nouns ***people*** referring to more than one person and ***police*** are always regarded as plural. However, when people can refer to a nation, race or religion, it is regarded as a singular noun, in which case it can take either a singular or plural form.

ex) People strongly argue that the police are to investigate the case.

They are an industrious people.

At university, she took a class on the history of the indigenous (native) peoples of Central and South America.

Exercise

Choose the correct answers for the following sentences.

1. 10% of the territory is / are covered with grass.

2. 70 percent of teachers say / says schools are not ready to protect students.

3. 35% of the syllables to which the subjects responded was / were segmented as two separate units.

4. What percentage of the people in Ethiopia is / are Muslim?

5. Approximately 45 of the population is / are Muslim.

6. The mayor as well as his brothers is / are going to prison.

7. Neither of the two traffic lights is / are working.

8. Which shirt do you want for Christmas? Either is / are fine with me.

9. Either my father or my brothers is / are going to sell the house.

10. Neither my brothers nor my father is / are going to sell the house.

11. Is / Are either my brothers or my father responsible?

12. Is / Are either my father or my brothers responsible?

13. My pants was / were torn.

14. A pair of plaid trousers is / are in the closet.

15. None of the engines is / are working.

16. None of the food is / are fresh.

17. None of the students has / have done their homework.

18. My assets was / were wiped out in the depression.

19. The average worker's earnings has / have gone up dramatically.

20. Our (My) thanks goes / go to the workers who supported the union.

21. Some of the voters is / are still angry.

22. A large percentage of the older population is / are voting against her.

23. Two-fifths of the troops was / were lost in the battle.

24. Two-fifths of the vineyard was / were destroyed by fire.

25. Forty percent of the students is / are in favor of changing the policy.

26. Forty percent of the student body is / are in favor of changing the policy.

27. Two and two is / are four.

28. The department members but not the chair has / have decided not to teach on Valentine's Day.

29. It is not the faculty members but the president who decide / decides this issue.

30. It was the speaker, not his ideas, that has / have provoked the students to riot.

31. Fifty thousand dollars is / are a lot of money.

32. Dollars is / are often used instead of rubles in Russia.

33. One-half of the faculty is / are retiring this summer.

34. One-half of the faculty has / have doctorates.

35. Fifty percent of the students has / have voted already.

12

INFINITIVE

12.1 Introduction

Infinitives are verb forms that serve as subject, complement, or object in a sentence. Their forms are shaped up with ***to*** + ***base form*** of the verb such as *'to speak' and 'to write'*. Unlike verbs tenses (e.g., speaks or wrote), infinitives do not usually specify the times of events or actions. In addition, their forms do not change depending on the subject, number or person.

12.2 Usage

1) SUBJECT: Infinitives can be used as the subject of a clause. In comtemporary English, ***it*** can be more often called as a grammatical (dummy) subject and thus infinitives tend to be placed toward the end of the clause.

ex) It is important to brush your teeth regularly.

It makes her happy to help others.

It is hard to please her.

To please her is hard. (= She is hard to please.)

2) SUBJECTIVE COMPLEMENT: After ***be-verb***, infinitives can serve as a subject complement, that is, a word or phrase which describes something about the subject.

ex) My job is to teach English.

She appeared to be worried about her health.

3) OBJECT: Infinitives can be used as the object of a clause. Particularly, infinitives can be adopted after verbs of feeling and thinking: decide, forget, hope, learn, love, plan, remember, or want.

ex) I like to watch movies on weekends.

He wants to become a doctor.

4) OBJECTIVE COMPLEMENT: Infinitives can act as an object complement after a direct object. A direct object and the infinitive directly follow some verbs (e.g., advise, encourage, order, remind, want, or intend).

ex) John advised me to see a doctor.

I asked him to leave me alone yesterday.

5) Infinitives can be often used after adjectives which express feelings and reactions.

ex) I was happy to receive the gift.
Kevin was shocked to hear the truth about her.
She is pleased to meet you.

6) ***Too*** can be used as an intensifier which expresses what is inadequate or excessive. The expression can be combined with an infinitive. Unlike ***too, Enough*** can express what is adequate and the expression can also be combined with an infinitive. In addition, the expressions (i.e., a lot, even, far, much, and still) that intensify comparatives also modify ***too***. Given this structure, ***for + object pronoun*** can be adopted. It is important to notice two possible meanings like the followings: I am too complicated to love - I am so complicated that I can't love someone vs. I am too complicated for anyone to love: I can't be loved.

ex) This spaghetti is too hot to eat.
He is far too old to get a job.
There was too much work to watch a movie.
My daughter is old enough to get a job.
She worked hard enough to buy a house.
My password is not secure enough for me to use (it).
This package is too heavy to lift.
This package is too heavy to lift it (x)

This package is too heavy for me to lift (it)

7) The structure ***for*** + ***noun/pronoun*** + ***to-infinitive*** can be used when an infinitive needs to have its own subject. It is important to note that the object of the proposition ***for*** acts as the subject of the infinitive.

ex) The question was difficult for me to answer.
Sarah will be happy for you to help her parents.

8) A negative infinitive can be used when the speaker has a clear plan/decision/determination in one's mind to avoid something; however, a negative verb when the speaker has no particular plan/decision/determination in one's mind to do something.

ex) Try not to outrun a dog. (Don't do that even though you could do that.)
Don't try to outrun a dog. (Don't make an attempt to do something you can't do.)

9) Infinitives can express a person's purpose. ***In order to*** or ***so as to*** can be adopted to represent a person's purpose.

ex) Paul has gone to finish his assignment.
I got up early in order to have breakfast.
We spoke quietly so as not to wake the baby.

10) Some adjectives (i.e., easy, difficult, good, and hard) can be placed with infinitives in a unique structure where the subject of the clause functionally acts as the object of the infinitive. The special structure sometimes finishes with a preposition. Given this case, object pronoun after the preposition or infinitives can be omitted. When the subject of the clause is really not the same as the object of the infinitives, ***easy, difficult, impossible,*** and so on cannot be employed in this structure.

ex) The recipe is easy to follow; It is easy to follow the recipe; To follow the recipe is easy.
This city is not a good place (for us) to live in.
This city is not a good place (for us) to live in it. (x)
Baseball is very exciting to play.
Baseball is very exciting to play it. (x)
I am difficult to make decisions. (x)
(I have difficulties (in) making decisions.)
The sofa is easy to scratch. (x)
(The sofa scratches easily.)

11) Infinitives can be employed in order to indicate something that people have to do. Both active and passive infinitive are possible. Active infinitives can be used if one is more concerned about the person who will perform the activity; however, passive infinitives can be used if one is more concerned about the activity, or the thing/person that the

activity is done to.

ex) She has sent me a paper to type.
Her desk is covered with papers to be typed up.
She hates to be talked about behind her back.

12) ***For* vs. *To-Infinitive* : Purpose**

12-1) Person's Purpose

For can be adopted to express a person's purpose to do something, only when a noun or noun phrase follows ***for.*** In conjunction with this view, ***for*** cannot be used before ***v-ing*** form, but a ***to-infinitive*** (***to*** + a base form of the verb) is adopted to indicate someone's purpose.

ex) He went to the company for an interview.
He went to the company for having an interview. (x)
He went to the company to have an interview.

12-2) The Purpose of an Object or Material

For can be employed before ***v-ing*** form to indicate the purpose of a thing: what it can be used for, especially when the subject of the clause is the thing. However, when the subject of the clause is a person, an infinitive is adopted to represent the purpose of an object or material.

ex) A thermometer is used for measuring temperature.
People use thermometers to measure temperature.

12-3) With Indefinite Pronouns

For + v-ing form can be employed after an indefinite pronoun such as *anything or something* in order to indicate the general purpose of a thing. On the other hand, a ***to-infinitive*** is more likely to be used to express a person's particular purpose.

ex) I need something for killing bugs.
(the general purpose of an object)
I need something to kill the/this/that bug.
(a person's particular purpose)
I need something to stop my headache.
(the subject of the infinitive).
Is there something/anything to drink in the refrigerator?
(the object of the infinitive)

13) Causative verbs (i.e., get, have, help, let, and make) can be used to talk about that somebody causes something (else) to occur and these verbs have unique grammatical structures as follows:

Get means 'persuading, encouraging or arranging for someone to do something.': ***Get + Someone + To-Infinitive***

ex) I got John to type the letter.
I got my secretary to check my schedule.

Have means 'asking or requesting someone to do something especially when to talk about giving orders and instructions.' Either ***Have + Someone + Bare Infinitive*** (the base form of verbs without ***to***) or ***Have + Something + Past Participle*** can be a possible structure.

ex) The doctor had the nurse take the patient's weight.
My teacher had our classroom painted.

Get vs. ***Have***: Compare the following two sentences
I had my secretary check my schedule. (I requested/asked for him/her to check my schedule.) vs.
I got my secretary to check my schedule. (At first, my secretary thought that it was not necessary to check my schedule, but I persuaded/encouraged/arranged him/her to check my schedule.)

Let means 'permitting or allowing something to happen.' ***Let + Someone/Something + Bare Infinitive*** can be a possible structure.

ex) The university let graduate students teach its undergraduate ones.
Parents should not let their children do whatever they want to do.

Help means 'assisting/aiding someone, or making it possible or easier for someone to do something.' ***Help + Someone + Bare Infinitive/To-Infinitive*** can be possible. Meanwhile, ***Cannot help + V-ing (gerund) or Cannot (help) but + Bare Infinitive*** can be used to talk about that someone cannot stop himself/herself (from) doing something.

ex) I helped my mother (to) set the table.
Teachers should help their students (to) achieve their academic goals.
He cannot help laughing when he saw my drawing.
I cannot (help) but accept your opinion on this matter.

Make means 'forcing or compelling someone to do something.' ***Make + Someone + Bare Infinitive*** can be a possible structure.

ex) Movies make us laugh and cry and find out the meaning in life.
You should make your body relax.

14) Perceptive verbs (i.e., feel, hear, listen, notice, observe, see, and watch) can be followed by ***Object + Bare Infinitive/ Present Participle.***

ex) I can see every star twinkle/twinkling on the hill.
I heard my mother call/calling my name.

Exercise

A. Decide if to-infinitives denote Subject (S), Complement (C), Object (O), Purpose (P), Obligation (OB), or Feeling (F).

1. I was disappointed to hear that the concert has been cancelled.

2. My brother got there early to get a good seat.

3. To travel around the world requires a lot of time and money.

4. Please let me know the names of the visitors to contact (be contacted).

5. We wanted to start a new business together.

6. The most important thing in life is to remain optimistic.

7. I got a paper application form to be submitted by next week.

8. We need to concentrate on reality, not what could have been.

9. I was happy to come to the end of my journey.

10. I have tried many ways to lose weight.

11. Maria decided not to be late for school again.

12. They were surprised to hear the accident yesterday.

13. It's important to keep the air clean.

14. My sister is planning to travel around the world for a year.

15. His dream is to be a famous fashion model.

16. Peter hopes to finish his physics homework as soon as possible.

17. The robber took out a knife to frighten the traveler.

18. I would like to thank you for attending the interview.

19. To visit the Great Pyramid is her lifelong dream.

20. The guard refused to let them enter the building.

B. Choose the correct answer.

1. My family is going to London to visit / for visiting my cousin.

2. This kitchen knife is especially useful to slice / for slicing vegetables.

3. We need to drop by the store on the way home for some bread / for buying some bread.

4. The smartphone is the most popular tool to navigate / for navigating numerous important life activities.

5. This medicine is used to treat / for treating symptoms caused by the common cold, allergies, or other breathing illnesses.

6. My parents always made me read / to read / reading a lot of books.

7. The coach watched the player kick / to kick / kicking the ball.

8. Maria helped her sister choose / to choose / choosing a smartphone.

9. I heard someone call / to call / calling my name from behind.

10. My teacher got us memorize / to memorize / memorizing a poem every week.

11. Mary had the mechanic check / to check / checking her brakes.

12. Peter had his car repair / to repair / repaired.

C. Identify the difference between the two sentences.

a. Don't try to laugh.

b. Try not to laugh.

13

GERUND

13.1 Introduction

A gerund is a word ending in '***-ing***' which is made from a verb, acting as the subject, the object, the complement of a sentence or the object of a preposition; that is, a gerund is considered to be functioning like a noun. A gerund usually takes a singular verb and sometimes may adopt a possessive to signify the agent of a gerund.

13.2 Usage

1) SUBJECT: Gerunds can operate as the subject of a sentence. A gerund phrase usually takes a singular verb. Two phrases connected with ***or*** or ***nor*** also take a singular verb. However, two gerund phrases connected with ***and*** take either a singular or plural verb.

ex) Learning English is important for many reasons.
Reading and listening to music are my hobbies.

2) OBJECT: Gerunds can also operate as the object of a sentence. Some verbs are generally followed by gerunds: *admit, avoid, consider, deny, dislike, enjoy, finish, mind, postpone, practice, and so on.*

ex) I enjoy walking in the rain.
Harry finished making a reservation in advance.
Our leader does not avoid taking responsibility for his actions.

3) COMPLEMENT: Gerunds can be adopted as the complement of a sentence.

ex) One of my duties is doing the dishes.
What he wants to do is travelling to other countries.

4) OBJECT of PREPOSITION: Gerunds can function as the object of a preposition. After a preposition, a gerund is normally used, not an infinitive.

ex) She usually tells a joke without laughing.
We're excited about being off work on Monday.

5) Some verbs can precede ***object* + *(from/in) -ing*** form: *deter, discourage, keep, prevent, spend, and stop.*

ex) The hot weather deterred my son (from) going out.
My parents tried to discourage me (from) being a singer.
His back injury kept him (from) playing in yesterday's game.
I could not prevent him (from) leaving the country.
Children spend their time (in) playing outside.
The snow did not stop us (from) enjoying the trip.

6) After some verbs such as *deserve, need, and require*, gerunds can have passive meanings. In addition, passive forms of ***-ing* *(being* + *past participle)*** are sometimes used to highlight that the agent or actor of the clause is being acted upon.

ex) Your proposals deserve discussing (deserve to be discussed)
This carpet needs cleaning. (needs to be cleaned)
The car requires repairing. (requires to be repaired)
My daughter enjoyed being taken to the amusement park.
He dislikes being interrupted.

7) Some phrasal verbs which have the word ***to*** as a preposition (i.e., be used *to*, in addition *to,* look forward *to*, or object *to*) must be followed by a gerund, not an infinitive.

ex) I'm used to working at night.
Amy is looking forward to seeing you soon.

8) Gerunds can be used with determiners such as *article* (i.e., the), *demonstrative adjective* (i.e., this, that) and *possessive* (i.e., my, his). It is important to notice that if who is being talked about (the subject/agent of a gerund) is quite clear and apparent, possessives and pronouns can be omitted.

ex) His arriving early was a wise decision.
The opening of the restaurant is coming soon.
Do you mind (my/me) opening the window?
The teacher disliked John's ***whispering*** in the class.
(Gerund: The teacher disliked the fact that John was whispering in the class; the object of *disliked* is John's whispering; the focal point is on *whispering*.)
The teacher disliked John ***whispering*** in the class.
(Present Participle as an adjective: The teacher disliked John who was whispering in the class; the object of *disliked* is John; the focal point is on *John*.)

9) Some verbs (i.e., advise, allow, forbid, permit, recommend or require) can be followed by either ***gerund or object (pronoun or noun phrase) + to-infinitive*** without a difference in meaning.

ex) My parents strongly advised me to sell my old car.
My parents strongly advised selling my old car.
He recommended writing a diary.
He recommended that I (should) write a diary.
He recommended me to write a diary.

He recommended the book to my students.
He recommended her to his friends.
She suggested buying a new house.
She suggested that I (should) buy a new house.
She suggested me to buy a new house. (x)
She suggested a new house to me.
She suggested me a new house. (x)

10) Some verbs can precede either a gerund or an infinitive with a change in meaning. ***Remember/Forget*** + ***gerund*** refers to the past when something that occurred in the past is remembered/forgotten. On the other hand, ***remember/forget*** + ***to-infinitive*** expresses the future when it is necessary for something to be remembered/forgotten.

ex) He'll never forget meeting her for the first time. (remember something he did in the past.); He still remembers meeting her for the first time.
Don't forget to bring my umbrella. (remember something you have to do in the future.); You should remember to bring my umbrella.

11) ***Regret*** + ***gerund*** refers back to the past with a disappointment. Unlike this, ***regret*** + ***to-infinitive*** can be used when the bad news has to be told someone.

ex) I regret cheating on the test - it was a stupid behavior to do so.

We regret to tell you that you have failed the test. (We are sorry to tell you the bad news about the results of the test.)

12) ***Like + gerund*** refers to real activities or actual experiences of finding something enjoyable or satisfactory (enjoyment or fondness), while ***Like + to-infinitive*** expresses potential activities or possible experiences about having a habitual preference or choice for something that one may not like or enjoy, but regard as being right, helpful or productive.

ex) I like swimming. (I enjoy swimming; I like what I experience in the real activity of swimming.)

I like to swim when it is hot. (I prefer/choose the option or possibility of swimming when it is hot; I like what happens during the potential activity of swimming when it is hot.)

I like to be honest. (It is right to be honest and I am; I think it is important to be honest.)

I like getting up early every day. (I enjoy getting up early every day; I like the experience of getting up early every day.)

I like to get up early in winter. (I prefer getting up early in winter, instead of oversleeping; It is useful/helpful to get up early in winter, even if I do not like or enjoy that.)

13) ***Stop*** + ***gerund*** expresses that an action in progress ends. ***Stop*** + ***to-infinitive*** interrupts an action in order to do something else.

ex) I stopped smoking. (I gave up smoking.)
I stopped to smoke. (I stopped in order to smoke.)

14) ***Try*** + ***gerund*** means '*to make an experiment (with different methods) to see what comes up.*' ***Try*** + ***to-infinitive*** means '*to make an attempt/effort to do something.' (even though it is difficult)*

ex) Try using butter instead of oil. (Use butter to see what will happen.)
Maria tries to lose weight. (Maria makes an effort to lose weight.)

13.3 Gerund vs. Present Participle

Both ***gerund*** and ***present participle*** end in ***-ing form***. But, each has a different function. A gerund functions like a noun (subject, object, and complement), while a present participle functions as an adjective. In addition, a gerund represents a fact or state at the moment of speaking, while a present participle represents something that is going on or in progress. Especially, perceptive verbs (i.e., see, smell, hear, listen to, and watch) are followed by ***noun/pronoun + present participle***.

ex) Jane is **walking** through the park.
(Present Participle: something is in progressive)
Do you know that man **driving** the car? (Present Participle: an adjective modifying the preceding noun, *that man*)
Eating late at night is bad for you.
(Gerund: the subject of the sentence)
He found her sitting on a bench in the park.
(Present Participle: the object complement of the sentence; When he arrived, she was sitting on a bench in the park.)
I caught someone **trying** to break the windows of my house.
(Present Participle: the object complement of the sentence; I caught someone who was trying to break the windows of my house.)
I saw John **walking** down the street.
(Present Participle: the object complement of the sentence; I saw John who was walking down the street.)

Exercise

A. Decide if the following sentences denote Subject (S), Complement (C), Object (O), or Object of Preposition (OP)

1. One of my hobbies is watching movies on weekends.

2. My wife suggested taking the children to the aquarium.

3. We talked about going to France for our vacation.

4. Eating plenty of vegetables helps reduce the risk of many diseases.

5. Would you mind speaking more slowly for me?

6. My brother stayed at home instead of attending class.

7. Preserving our cultural heritage is of utmost importance.

B. Choose the correct answer.

1. He remembers going / to go to the beach when he was a child.

2. The company regrets informing / to inform employees that the New York office will close next month.

3. The doctors tried saving / to save her life but she died.

4. Don't forget meeting / to meet Tom at 9 o'clock this evening.

5. On the way to Osaka, we stopped looking / to look at an old tree.

6. Why don't you try using / to use butter instead of oil?

7. Andrew regrets spending / to spend so much money yesterday.

8. We have stopped using / to use shampoo and conditioner for two months.

9. I'll never forget traveling / to travel abroad for the first time.

10. This security system prevents robbers entering / to enter the house.

11. Many people put off going / to go to the dentist because of their fear of treatment.

12. Sophia began playing / to play the violin when she was five.

13. We plan living / to live in a small town in the near future.

14. This movie is really long, but it is worth watching / to watch.

15. I need sleeping / to sleep at least eight hours a night.

16. My worries kept me sleeping / to sleep properly.

17. My mother loves watching / to watch soap operas on television.

18. Please remember locking / to lock the door when you leave.

19. Jason usually avoids expressing / to express his opinions.

20. I asked my secretary copying / to copy this letter for me.

21. She is used to do / doing several jobs at the same time.

22. The counselor advised her expressing / to express her emotions.

23. My parents object to have / having pets at home.

24. I am looking forward to hear / hearing good news from you.

25. Would you mind opening / to open the window?

26. My sister likes watching / to watch movies when she gets some rest.

27. Sarah likes eating / to eat vegetables.

28. When my friends visit me, I like making / to make some cookies.

14

NOUN CLAUSE

14.1 Introduction

A noun clause is a dependent clause that contains a subject and a verb phrase. In addition, a noun clause functions like a noun as the subject, object, and complement of a sentence. A noun clause cannot stand alone in a sentence since this is always a dependent clause.

14.2 Usage

1) A ***that***-clause can function as the subject, object, and complement of a sentence. If a ***that***-clause as the subject is too long, the introductory (grammatical/dummy) subject, ***'it'*** can be used. ***'It'*** typically stands in the position of the subject, which merely introduces that a ***that***-clause follows the grammatical/dummy subject ***'it.'***

ex) They denied that Jack had stolen the purse.
It was obvious to me that the boys were lying.

2) A noun clause can also start with ***a question word*** (i.e., who, what, which, when, where, why, and how), which contains a subject and a verb phrase. The word order of the ***wh***-clause is ***'Wh-question word + subject + verb.'*** The noun clause with a question word operates as the subject, object, and complement of a sentence.

ex) Where we travel depends on our budget.
Please tell me what you want to eat.
The problem was how I should apologize to her.

3) Question words (i.e., who, which, what, when, where, and how) can precede ***a to-infinitive***. The question words followed by infinitives can function as a noun clause and express what ***can/could*** or ***should*** be done. However, it is important to notice that ***why*** cannot be operating in this way.

ex) We must remember where to get off. (where we should get off)
I will show you how to use chopsticks.
(how you can or should use chopsticks)
I can't decide which to buy. (which one I should buy)
I don't know what to do. (what I can or should do)

4) A noun clause with ***whoever***, ***whatever***, or ***whichever*** can be the subject or object of a sentence. ***Whoever*** means anyone who + V, ***whatever/whichever*** means anything that S + V. The clause with ***whoever***, ***whatever***, or ***whichever*** takes a singular verb.

ex) Whatever she says is not true.
Whoever leaves last should lock the door.
Whichever brand you prefer is fine with me.
Let me know whichever of the two dates is more favorable to you.

5) **Whether vs. If**

A noun clause which begins with ***whether*** or ***if*** is to deliver the idea of alternative options. ***If*** and ***whether*** can be employed interchangeably with no meaning change; however, ***whether*** is more often used than ***if*** in formal English when introducing alternatives.

5-1) ***Whether*** or ***if*** can be adopted in a sentence which focuses on alternatives: ***whether*** is more often used in order to express alternatives (yes or no / X or Y), but ***if*** is less commonly employed to introduce alternatives.

ex) She asked me if I had reserved a room.
She asked whether I had reserved one or two rooms.
I wondered if you could help me.

5-2) In the placement of the object of a preposition, only ***whether*** should be used instead of ***if.***

ex) We'd like to talk about whether you are going to New York. (o)
We'd like to talk about if you are going to New York. (x)

5-3) ***Whether*** can be used before an infinitive with alternatives, but ***if*** cannot precede an infinitive with alternatives.

ex) I can't decide whether to go out or stay at home tomorrow. (o)
I can't decide if to go out or stay at home tomorrow. (x)

5-4) ***If*** cannot be placed at the beginning of a sentence when it comes to alternative options; in the case of a conditional statement, ***if*** can appear at the beginning of a sentence. However, ***whether (or not)*** is usually located at the beginning of a sentence when introducing alternatives.

ex) Whether he is alive after the aircraft accident is not known. (o)
If he is alive after the aircraft accident is not known. (x)

5-5) When expressing an alternative, ***or not*** can often be paired with ***whether*** and ***if***. With ***whether***, ***or not*** can be placed at the end of a sentence or immediately after ***whether,*** but with ***if***, ***or not*** can be placed only at the end of a sentence.

ex) I don't know whether or not Maria passed her exam. (o)

I don't know whether Maria passed her exam or not. (o)

I don't know if or not Maria passed her exam. (x)

I don't know if Maria passed her exam or not. (o)

Exercise

A. Identify the answers of the sentences below.

1. Researchers are interested in whether / if a new drug is effective.

2. We would like to know whether / if you have any experience in teaching.

3. The question is whether / if or not he is qualified to be a candidate.

4. We can't decide whether / if to invest in business or real estate.

5. Whether / If she likes me is my biggest concern.

6. I want to talk with you about whether / if you are going to attend the meeting.

7. It is not easy to decide whether / if to quit my job or not.

8. It does't matter whether / if you agree with me or not.

9. I don't care whether / if people like me or dislike me.

10. We asked Jack whether / if he planned to join our team or not.

11. Eric doesn't know whether / if the answer is right or wrong.

12. Our plan depends on whether / if you can borrow your mother's car or not.

13. We discussed whether / if to raise a dog or not.

14. Whether / If or not we go to France for our holiday depends on the cost.

15. They are confused about whether / if they want kids or not.

16. I would like to know whether / if you want wine or beer.

17. Think about whether / if you really want to marry him or not.

18. I don't remember whether / if I turned off the oven.

19. Whether / If you come with me or not will not change my decision.

20. There was an argument about whether / if we should sell the house.

21. Customers will choose whatever / whichever / whoever product is cheaper.

22. We can go on Friday or Saturday, whatever / whichever / whoever you prefer.

23. Say whatever / whichever / whoever you need.

24. Whatever / Whichever / Whoever wants to join us will be welcome.

25. You can drive whatever / whichever / whoever of the cars you want.

B. Combine the following two sentences into one sentence.

1. I don't understand. Why is my girlfriend angry at me?

2. Anyone wants to participate in the show. He needs to visit our website.

3. Maria trusts me blindly. She believes everything that I say.

4. My young daughter wants to know. How long will she stay in the hospital?

5. Do you think? What makes her happy?

6. Can you tell me? Where can I find the hospital?

7. Do you believe? When can you afford to buy the house?

8. Do you think? Why did Michael quit the school?

9. Can you guess? When did she meet her client?

10. Do you think? Who is the most suitable person for that position?

15
Adjectival Clause

15.1 Introduction

An adjectival clause begins with ***a relative pronoun*** (i.e., that, which, and who) or ***a relative adverb*** (i.e., when, where, and why) in order to identify and add more information about people or things. As a result, an adjectival clause is also referred to as ***'a relative clause.'*** Equally important, a relative pronoun or adverb, which functions as a conjunction, links an adjectival clause to an antecedent. For example, in the sentence 'This is the house that (which) my grandfather built,' ***'the house'*** is the antecedent and ***'that (which)'*** is the relative pronoun.

15.2 Usage

1) When ***who, whom,*** and ***which*** introduce an adjectival (relative) clause, ***who(m)*** refers to *people*, and ***which*** refers to *things or*

animals (sometimes, ***who*** may refer to *animals* under the condition that one identifies the gender of the animals). ***Who(m)*** and ***which*** can function as the subject or the object of an adjectival clause. ***Whom*** is more commonly used in a formal style. Meanwhile, ***which*** sometimes refer to a preceding whole clause or sentence

ex) I want to be a politician who(m) many people respect.
This is the cat which was hit by a bicycle.
She deleted the files, which made me angry.
He seemed more nervous than usual, which was because he was about to have a job interview soon.

2) ***That*** can be used in an adjectival clause instead of ***who(m)*** or ***which*** to refer to people, things and animals. ***That*** can operate as the subject or object of an adjectival clause. Especially, an object relative pronoun (that, who(m), which) can often be omitted. ***That*** can also be used with quantity expressions such as all, any(thing), every(thing), and no(thing).

ex) I don't like the picture that hung in the living room.
This is the book (that) I bought yesterday.
We should not believe everything that we watch on T.V.

3) A relative pronoun can operate as the object of a preposition. In a formal style, the preposition comes immediately before the relative pronoun, but in an informal style, it comes at the end of a relative clause.

ex) My sister met a man with whom I used to work.
The house which Mozart was born in has been well preserved.

4) **Whose**

4-1) ***Whose*** is a relative possessive pronoun, which can be used before nouns in place of possessive pronouns such as *her, his, its, or their.* ***Whose*** can refer back to people or things. In an adjectival clause, ***whose*** + ***noun*** can be the subject, object of a verb, or the object of a preposition. Instead of ***whose*** + ***noun***, ***noun*** + ***of which*** can often be commonly used in order to indicate things, but, ***of which...*** + ***noun*** is occasionally possible.

ex) The grand prize will go to the director **whose film** shows the most excitement and imagination.
The grand prize will go to the director **the film of which** shows the most excitement and imagination.
He's directed a film **whose name** I've not remembered.
He's directed a film **the name of which** I've not remembered.

He's directed a film **of which the name** I've not remembered.

He's directed a film **of which** I've not remembered **the name**.

He's directed a film **which (that)** I've not remembered **the name of**.

4-2) ***Whose*** replaces a possessive personal (animate) or inanimate noun, but ***of which*** can only replace a possessive inanimate noun in an adjectival clause. In addition, quantity phrases with ***which [whom, whose]***, such as ***most [all, some, one] of which [whom, whose]***, are located at the front of an adjectival clause, which comes immediately after the noun that the adjectival clause modifies.

ex) The Lotte World, **all of which** belongs to the Lotte Company, is located in Seoul.

The choice of medication depends on a variety of factors, **one of which** is the pattern of symptoms.

Jack has read five books since last month, **some of which** are really informative for him.

The pyramids in Egypt, **most of which** were built thousands of years ago, have many different shapes and sizes.

In Britain, there are approximately 3 million color blind people, **most (the majority) of whom** are male.

We have three children, **all of whom** are majoring in architecture.

I have met lots of musicians, **some of whom** are musically gifted.

The students, **one of whom** is supposed to graduate this semester, failed the final exam.

I argued with my parents last night, **some of whose** remarks offended me.

Monet is one of the greatest artists, **most of whose** works were inspired by the natural beauty.

5) Relative adverbs such as ***when***, ***where***, and ***why*** can be used to add up the descriptive information such as *time, place, or reason*. ***When*** refers to ***time***; ***'at/on/in/during which,'*** ***where*** refers to ***place***; ***'at/on/in which,'*** and ***why*** refers to ***reason***: ***'for which.'*** Therefore, the relative adverbs each can be replaced by ***a preposition + a relative pronoun***.

ex) This is the shop **where** I bought my flowers.

This is the shop **in which** I bought my flowers.

I don't know the reason **why** Amy was not in class yesterday.

I don't know the reason **for which** Amy was not in class yesterday.

The 1990s were the decade **when** wide-leg pants were considered fashionable.

The 1990s were the decade **in/during which** wide-leg pants were considered fashionable.

6) There are two types of relative clauses: ***a restrictive (identifying) clause*** and ***a non-restrictive (non-identifying) clause***. The restrictive clause modifies the antecedent by adding up essential information as well as specifying the antecedent. No commas are employed to activate the clause. Unlike the restrictive clause, the non-restrictive clause provides extra/supplementary information about the antecedent that is already known by its name or by its shared context or knowledge. ***That*** cannot be used in the non-restrictive clause, and commas are employed before and after the clause.

ex) He married a woman that he met at a party.

The Golden Gate Bridge, which is one of the landmarks of San Francisco, is the second longest suspension bridge in the U.S.

Exercise

Select the correct relative pronouns for the following sentences.

1. My car, ______ I bought last year, needs a new steering wheel.

    a. that
    b. which
    c. whose
    d. whom

2. Do you know the boy ______ is talking to Linda now?

    a. which
    b. what
    c. of which
    d. who

3. French is a language ______ I have found hard to pronounce.

    a. who
    b. that
    c. whose
    d. where

4. The day ______ Korea became independent was August 15th, 1945.

   a. whose
   b. when
   c. what
   d. why

5. The student ______ phone was just stolen was very upset.

   a. whose
   b. that
   c. when
   d. who

6. Jack, _____ just graduated from middle school, is an accomplished hockey player.

   a. that
   b. which
   c. who
   d. whose

7. I sent my job applications to several companies, ______ were rejected.

   a. whose
   b. most of which

c. some of whom

d. they

8. Over 3000 people, ______ came from around the world, attended the ceremony.

a. some of which

b. some of them

c. all of them

d. most of whom

9. The little girl had a Barbie doll, ______ arms were missing.

a. both of whose

b. both of which

c. both of who

d. both of whom

10. The writer, ______ book has been recently published, delivered a lecture in front of a big audience.

a. which

b. whose

c. who

d. his

11. That picture was taken at the restaurant ______ I used to go.

a. when
b. who
c. what
d. where

12. I will never forget the day ______ you proposed to me.

a. on which
b. which
c. where
d. what

13. I met an old friend of mine, ______ didn't recognize me at first.

a. he
b. who
c. whom
d. whose

14. This program is particularly good for students ______ second language is English.

a. which
b. whose

c. who

d. whom

15. Elephants, ______ are the largest land mammals, live in herds of 10 or more adults.

a. which

b. who

c. what

d. that

16. He left early, ________ was wise.

a. which

b. who

c. what

d. that

17. She seemed more talkative than usual, _____ was because she was nervous.

a. which

b. who

c. what

d. that

18. They think I sit around drinking coffee all day. _____, of course, I do.

a. which
b. who
c. what
d. that

19. It may rain tomorrow, in _____ case we will have to stay indoors.

a. which
b. who
c. what
d. that

20. She refused to listen to me, at _____ point I decided to leave.

a. which
b. who
c. what
d. that

21. I know many foreign students, ______ are able to speak English.

a. most of whom
b. some of them

c. most of which
d. none of them

22. Every cosmetic may contain chemicals, ________ cause irritations or allergic reactions.

a. most of them
b. all of whom
c. some of which
d. whose

23. My favorite author is Alain de Botton, ______ books are well known by the public.

a. his
b. some of his
c. most of which
d. most of whose

24. There are more than 285 million blind people in the world, ______ suddenly lost their sight.

a. they
b. some of them
c. some of that
d. some of whom

25. Their marriage lasted five years, __________ time the couple had two children, John and Marry.

a. on which
b. in which
c. during which
d. when

26. My passport cannot be used anymore because the period _________ it was valid is over.

a. on which
b. at which
c. during which
d. when

16

Adverbial Clause

16.1 Introduction

An adverbial clause is a dependent clause that operates as adverbs. Since an adverbial clause cannot stand alone, it must start with a subordinating conjunction (i.e., although, because, if, and when) to link a dependent clause to an independent clause in order to provide explanatory details.

16.2 Usage

TIME

Be noticed that in an adverbial clause of time, the simple present tense is used in order to refer to the future event.

1) ***Before*** represents the event that occurs before an event in the independent clause. ***After*** represents the event that occurs after an event in the independent clause.

ex) I met him just before he left the office.
She went to work after she fed the dogs.

2) ***When*** and ***as*** represent ***'at that moment/time'***; therefore, these conjunctions take a dependent clause where an event interrupts another event (of short duration) that is in progress. In addition, the dependent clause shows simultaneous activities (= at the same time) and sometimes introduce an event that occurs immediately before the event in the independent clause.

ex) As/When I called, she was having dinner (interruption).
As/When he was walking down the hill, he saw his brother crossing the road (at the same time).
When I opened the door, the cat jumped in (immediately after).
When the new restaurant opens, we'll have lunch there to celebrate my mother's birthday (present tense for a future event).

3) Both ***while*** and ***as*** represent ***'during that time'*** to describe two activities or situations of long duration at the same time and they are often paired with the past progress because ***'during that time'*** signifies an ongoing activity. Of particular interest

are two usages of ***as***, which means ***when*** for activities of short duration and ***while*** for events or situations of long duration as well.

ex) While I was taking a shower. she was doing the dishes.
She watched TV while I was out.
As the children were sleeping on the couch, she talked/was talking on the phone.
As he grows up, he becomes more realistic.

4) ***By the time*** is followed by a clause in which an event occurs or happens possibly before and up to X time (=between past/present/future and X time).

ex) By the time I got to the movie theater, the film had already started. (= the film started between a particular past time and the time we arrived there; My car broke down on the way to the movie theater last night. It took me a long time to get there and the film started during this time.)
I will have finished my assignment by the time you arrive. (= between now and the time you arrive)
[from a package note] Our summer break ends tomorrow. So by the time you receive this package, we will get back to school.
(= between tomorrow and the time you receive this package)

5) ***Since*** expresses ***'from that time'*** and it precedes a noun phrase or a clause with a starting time, or a specific time for an event. ***Since*** is usually paired with the present perfect or present perfect progressive.

ex) I have been playing piano since the age of five.
(my early childhood; a noun phrase)
She has been very busy since she got a new job. (a clause)
We haven't even seen her since June 2010. (a specific time)

6) ***Until*** and ***till*** represent ***'up to that time'*** and they deliver an idea of how long a state or situation continues up. Both ***until*** and ***till*** can be used with the simple past or simple present. ***Till*** is commonly used in informal English.

ex) I walked around till it got dark.
We'll wait with you until the taxi comes.

7) ***As soon as*** can be used when the one activity occurs immediately after the other activity.

ex) As soon as she heard the news, she called him.
As soon as I hold my doctoral degree, I will teach.

8) ***Whenever*** and ***every time*** can represent repetitive and habitual activities, which mean ***'each time something occurs.'***

ex) We make a pie every time he visits.
Whenever I go to Paris, I stay with my sister.

CAUSE AND EFFECT

1) ***Because*** represents a reason (cause) for the result (effect) stated in the independent clause. When placing more stress on the (unknown) reason, ***because*** is more commonly used and informal than ***since*** and ***as***.

ex) I was angry with Sally because she was late.
Just because I don't usually smile, people think I'm very grumpy and picky.

2) ***Since*** and ***as*** expresses the same as ***because***, but ***since*** and ***as*** can often be used to express a known reason or put more emphasis on the effect (result) than the cause (reason).

ex) You can go out and play since you have finished all your homework.
Since Thursday is a holiday, we don't need to go to school.
John wore his rain boots as it was raining.

3) ***Now that*** states ***'because now.'*** ***Now that*** can be used to talk about the reasons for present or future circumstances.

ex) Now that we have finished the exam, let's go camping.
Now that the weather is getting warmer, the children want to play outside all day.

CONTRAST

1) ***Although*** and ***though***, which refer to ***'in spite of/despite the fact that'*** can be used to introduce a dependent clause (X) that makes an independent clause (Y) unexpected and surprising: the idea of X is contradictory to that of Y. ***Although*** and ***though*** can be interchangeably used, but ***although*** is more formal than ***though***. ***Although*** and ***though*** are less empathic than ***Even though***.

ex) Even though it was expensive, (= In spite of the fact that it was expensive) I bought the brand new laptop.
We still feel hungry (al)though we just had dinner. (= despite the fact that we just had dinner)

2) ***While*** and ***whereas*** introduce a dependent clause which is in direct contrast to the situation in an independent clause; however, the two ideas do not contradict each other.

ex) Whereas Susan is good at English, her sister is absolutely hopeless.
I like to live in the countryside, while my husband prefers to live in the city.

3) The ***WH***-words (i.e., whoever, whatever, whichever, however, whenever, and wherever) can function as adverbial clauses to express the sense of ***no matter who/what/which/how/when/where***-clause.

ex) Whatever you decide, I will support you.
Whenever I go to Canada, I visit my sister.
Whoever wins the game, we will totally accept the results.
However long it takes, I'll never give up.
Wherever we travel, the weather is always bad.
Whichever route you take, it takes about two hours.

4) ***Despite*** and ***in spite of*** are prepositions which are followed by noun phrases or gerunds. They express the sense of ***'contrast'*** which links unexpected/surprising information to the independent clause. In other words, both ***despite*** and ***in spite of*** refer to contrary reasoning. ***In spite of*** is less formal than ***despite.***

ex) We went hiking despite the hot weather.
I enjoy my job in spite of the low salary.

CONDITION

Be noticed that in an adverbial clause of condition, the present simple tense is used in order to refer to the future time.

1) ***If***-clauses represent the possible conditions required for the results; these clauses introduce expected outcomes based on the condition (true situation).

ex) If the weather improves, I will go on a picnic.
If you get enough sleep, you will get better.

2) ***Whether***-clauses express that either one condition or the other does not matter; the outcome will not change.

ex) We are going to go hiking tomorrow whether or not it is hot.

Whether she wants or not, she'll have to wash the dishes.

3) ***Even if***-clauses are quite similar to ***whether***-clauses in meaning; In particular, ***even if***-clauses can often be used to talk about untrue (unreal) or imaginary situations (events) in the future and their probable results. The imaginary situations on which the speaker'/writer's decisions (the probable results) are based are only possibilities: something in an ***even if*** clause might happen, but it not certain.

ex) We're supposed to go on a field trip even if it rains. (= whether or not it rains)

Even if I become a billionaire, (an unreal/imaginary situation) I will always live a plain and simple life. (a probable result)

4) ***In case***-clauses refer to precautions, which are done in order to be prepared for possible future circumstances; ***in case*** expresses the idea of ***'if something happens by chance.'***

ex) In case he dies without heirs, his money will go to charity. (NOT In case he will die...; = If by chance he happens to die)

I took/have taken cash (just) in case we (should) need it at the museum. (= ... if we happen to need cash at the museum by chance)

5) ***Unless***-clauses express the sense of '***if...not*** or ***except if.***' ***Unless***-clauses indicate that if an action in an ***unless***-clause does not occur first, the other one in an independent clause will occur.

ex) Unless you hurry up, we will not arrive in time.
Unless you're listening to the radio, I will turn it off.

6) ***As long as*** and ***so long as*** are mainly used to express the idea of ***'on condition that or provided that.' As long as*** may also express the time when to compare two situations with a similar length of time or duration.

ex) I will lend him some money as/so long as he repays it.
(= ...provided/on condition that he repays it.)
You can stay at my house as long as you want.
The conference lasted as long as three hours/the tennis match.

16.3 In Case vs. If

In case can not be used as an alternative to ***if. 'Do X in case Y occurs'*** expresses the sense of ***'Do X (first) because Y occurs or might occur later.'*** Unlike this, ***'Do X if Y occurs'*** expresses the idea of ***'Do X (later) after Y occurs or might occur.'***

ex) We'll buy some eggs in case the guests come.
(= Let's buy some eggs now because they might come later.)
We'll buy some eggs if the guests come.
(= Let's wait and see what happens. If the guests come, then let's buy some eggs. If they don't come, we won't.)

16.4 Unless vs. If...not

Both ***unless*** and ***if... not*** express the idea of '***except if.***' When the meaning of ***if... not*** leans toward ***'because...not,' unless*** cannot be used.

ex) I'll meet you this afternoon at 2 pm - unless my airplane is late.
(=... if my bus isn't late/except if my airplane is late.)
My parents will be disappointed if I do not pass the exam.
(NOT... unless I get home by 10 pm.)

(= They will be disappointed because I do not pass the exam.)

16.5 Until vs. By

Until can represent the idea of how long a situation or state continues up. ***By*** can express an idea of a deadline of an event or activity (= at or before X time; not later than X time).

ex) You need to stay in bed until tomorrow morning. (NOT by tomorrow morning)
You need to go to bed by 9 pm. (at or before 9 pm.; not later than 9 pm.; NOT until 9 pm.)

16.6 Until vs. Before

Until/till can be similar to ***before.*** Both ***until*** and ***before*** represent something earlier than a particular activity and specific time, and refer to the time when a particular situation, activity, or period ends.

ex) I won't be seeing Nancy until/before Friday.
There are only about four weeks left until/before Thanksgiving Day.

16.7 But vs. However

But or ***however*** can be used to introduce the statement that contrasts with something which has just been said. However, ***but*** and ***however*** are not interchangeable because they are distinctive in terms of form.

ex) I want to travel the world, but I don't have enough money.
I want to travel the world. However, I don't have enough money.
She studied hard, but she failed in the exams.
She studied hard; however, she failed in the exams.

But is a conjunction; it links two clauses. Unlike this, ***however*** is an adverb; ***however*** joins two clauses semantically, not grammatically. This is why ***however*** is followed by a period or semicolon. Unlike ***but***, ***however*** can stand in diverse placements.

ex) However, this book is not a good choice for beginners.
This book, however, is not a good choice for beginners.
This book is not a good choice for beginners, however.

16.8 By the time vs. When

By the time precedes a clause in which an event emerges or happens possibly before and up to the X time. In other words, ***by the time*** expresses that an event occurs between past/present/future and X time. On the other hand, ***when*** indicates the time when an event happens at X time.

ex) By the time you arrive, I will bake a cake.
(= I will bake a cake between now and the time you arrive; before or up to the time you arrive.)
When you arrive, I will bake a cake.
(= I will bake a cake at the time you arrive.)

16.9 When vs. If

When represents more sureness/certainty than ***if***. One can use ***when*** to say that someone is sure that something will occur in the future. However, one can use ***if*** to say that someone is unsure about whether something will happen or not in the future.

ex) I'll see you when I finish work. (= I'm certain to finish my work.)
I'll see you If I finish work. (= Maybe I'll finish work, maybe not.)

When ***if*** and ***when*** refer to the idea of ***'every time that'*** or ***'whenever'***, both can be used without a difference in meaning.

ex) When/If you boil water, it will kill much of bacteria.
(= Whenever/Every time that...)

16.10 Even Though vs. Even If

Even though refers to ***'in spite of/despite the fact that'*** and it is mainly used to talk about real situations. ***Even if***, on the other hand, refers to ***'whether or not'*** and it is usually used to say what would happen in the untrue (unreal) or imaginary (improbable) future situations.

Compare:

Even though he is a billionaire (a real situation), he lives a plain and simple life. (the unexpected/surprising idea contrast to the real situation) [= In spite of/Despite the fact that he is a millionaire, he lives a plain and simple life.]
Even if he becomes a billionaire (an unreal/imaginary situation), he will always live a plain and simple life. (a probable result) [= If there is even a possibility that he'll become a billionaire...]

16.11 Because of vs. Due to

Because of cannot be substituted for ***due to*** or vice versa. This is because that ***because of*** is rooted in an adverb, but ***due to*** is rooted in an adjective. Therefore, ***because of*** functions as an adverbial prepositional phrase, but ***due to*** functions as an adjectival prepositional phrase: to be more precise, ***because of*** describes or restricts the verb phrases, but, ***due to*** describes or restricts the noun phrases.

ex) His loss of appetite was due to a headache. (o)
His loss of appetite was because of a headache. (x)
He lost his appetite due to a headache. (x)
He lost his appetite because of a headache. (o)

16.12 Punctuation: Colon, Semi-Colon, and Dash

Colon

1) A colon (:) can be used to explain further and specific details: it adds up additional information on the first sentence.

ex) Kevin had to see a doctor: he had a bad cold.
I was happy today: I got a present from my brother.

2) A colon (:) can be used to present a list and then, two sentences are on the same thought.

ex) We bought some vegetables at the grocery store: cabbage, broccoli, cucumber, and asparagus.
The price includes the following: flight to Paris, hotel accommodation and tourist tax.

3) A colon (:) can be used to introduce direct speech, or especially cite the quotation.

ex) She said: "You have to see a doctor as soon as possible."
MACBETH: "Fair is foul, and foul is fair."

Semi-Colon

1) A semi-colon (;) can be used to semantically link the two clauses which are grammatically independent: a semi-colon is functionally placed somewhere in between a comma and a period. That, it is stronger than a comma, but weaker than a period.

ex) Call me tomorrow; we can decide whether to go out or not then.
My doctor told me to avoid fast food; nevertheless, I ate two hamburgers with a coke.

2) A semi-colon (;) can also be used to present a series of separate items in a list.

ex) During my trip around Europe, I've visited Paris, France; Berlin, Germany; and Rome, Italy.
Yesterday I met Maria, who is short; Peter, who is a psychology major; and Eric, who has curly hair.

Dash

In informal writing, dashes (-) can be used instead of colons or semi-colons.

ex) Don't forget to bring your belongings-towel, toothbrush and toothpaste.
You had better not eat too much-you will have to go on a diet.

Exercise

A. Choose the correct answer.

1. I will pay off some of my debt _______ the end of this year.

   a. until
   b. while
   c. by
   d. before

2. I will give you my number _______ you need to contact me.
   (= I will give you my number because you might need it later.)

   a. in case
   b. while
   c. but
   d. if

3. You will damage your health _______ you quit drinking alcohol.

   a. if
   b. as long as
   c. unless
   d. when

4. _______ she was dressed up, we assumed she was going on a date.

a. Although
b. After
c. Because of
d. Since

5. We can not wait _______ the holidays begin.

a. until
b. by
c. for
d. during

6. I spoke quietly _______ I didn't want Jonathan to hear.

a. because of
b. due to
c. because
d. as long as

7. I met her _______ I was staying in London last year.

a. whenever
b. while
c. during
d. despite

8. _______ I finish college, I will have passed my driving test. (= I will pass the test between now and the time I finish college.)

a. While
b. When
c. By the time
d. As

9. The program was canceled _______ the rain.

a. due to
b. despite
c. for
d. because of

10. She likes to eat out _______ I prefer to eat at home.

a. however
b. as
c. when
d. while

11. We'd like to attend the party, _______ we already have plans this weekend.

a. but
b. in spite of

c. however

d. while

12. I sold the house _______ it was against my parents' wills.

a. because

b. although

c. since

d. despite

13. All assignments must be received _______ the end of this month.

a. by

b. after

c. until

d. when

14. _______ we were eating breakfast, someone knocked on the door.

a. Since

b. For

c. While

d. During

15. My brother will be here tonight, _______ his flight is delayed.

a. as long as
b. by the time
c. if
d. unless

16. _______ I have gotten a driver's license, I am going to buy a new car.

a. Although
b. Now that
c. While
d. Unless

17. _______ gossips to you, s/he will gossip about you.

a. Whoever
b. Whichever
c. Wherever
d. Whenever

18. Nobody will believe Mary _______ she tells the truth.

a. as long as
b. even though
c. even if
d. since

19. The success of the restaurant was _______ its new manager.

a. because of
b. due to
c. for
d. until

20. They didn't lose hope _______ the terrible tsunami destroyed everything.

a. even if
b. because
c. since
d. even though

21. There is only about one hour _______ the meeting.

a. before
b. as
c. however
d. until

22. The job wasn't very interesting. _______ the pay was good.

a. Although
b. However
c. But
d. Since

23. The doctors couldn't save her _______ all of his efforts.

a. in spite of
b. because of
c. due to
d. despite of

24. You can have a cat _______ you promise to take care of it.

a. while
b. before
c. as long as
d. even though

25. _______ Eric felt thirsty, he quickly drank two glasses of water.

a. Since
b. Even if
c. Unless
d. In case

26. We will buy a bottle of wine _______ the guests stay long.

a. in case
b. while
c. but
d. if

27. We have bought a bottle of wine _____ the guests stay long.

a. in case
b. while
c. but
d. if

28. Please write down my address _______ you don t want to forget it.

a. in case
b. while
c. but
d. if

29. He wrote down her phone number _________ he should forget it.

a. in case
b. while
c. but
d. if

B. Fill in the blanks with correct punctuation marks.

1. Whales are not fish (   ) they are warm-blooded mammals.

2. There are four types of blood (   ) A, B, AB and O.

3. We have agreed on the outcome (   ) male participants perform better than do female participants.

4. We will go to the zoo next weekend (   ) Sunday mornings aren't that crowded.

5. I hate to eat vegetables (   ) they are usually bitter.

6. The flight attendant said (   ) "Ladies and Gentlemen, please fasten your seatbelts."

7. I recommend you this book Oak Furniture (   ) the Spanish Tradition.

8. Michael has gone to the party (   ) Amy has gone to sleep.

9. My favorite authors and books are Michael Sandel, What Is Justice ( ) Alvin Toffler, Future Shock ( ) and Paulo Coelho, The Alchemist.

10. My boss did not accept the plan ( ) consequently, she suggested several changes.

17

HYPOTHETICAL IF

17.1 Introduction

A ***if***-clause can express a counter-factual situation that is unlikely to happen, or is imaginary or unreal. In doing so, a past tense or past perfect aspect can be used in the ***if***-clause and a modal verb (i.e., could, might and would) can be used in the independent clause.

17.2 Usage

1) Counter-Factual Present/Future (Untrue in the Present/Future)
   In order to describe a present or future situation that is improbable or is not going to be real, a ***past tense*** can be used in the ***if***-clause, and ***would (could/ might)*** + ***bare infinitive*** can be used in the independent clause.

ex) If I had enough money, I would buy the house. (= In reality, I don't have enough money now so I can't buy the house.)
If I have enough money, I will buy the house. (true situation in the present; there is an open and high possibility.)
If I had enough money, I bought the house. (true situation in the past; there was an open and high possibility.)
If I weren't at work, I would/could be on the beach. (= In reality, I am at work so I can't be on the beach.)

2) Counter-Factual Past (Untrue in the Past)
A ***past perfect aspect*** can be employed in the ***if***-clause, and ***would (could/might) have + p.p.*** can be employed in the independent clause, in order to describe a past event or situation that did not occur and to depict what possibly turned out in the past.

ex) If I had studied harder, I could have passed the exam. (= In reality, I didn't study hard so I didn't pass the exam.)
If he had taken a taxi, he wouldn't have been late for the meeting.
(= In reality, he didn't take a taxi so he was late for the meeting.)

3) In a mixed hypothetical (conditional) sentence, the time in the ***if***-clause does not correspond to the time in the independent clause. There are two types of mixed conditional sentences:

3-1) One is that the past perfect aspect is used in the ***if***-clause and then ***would (could/might) + bare infinitive*** is used in the independent clause. The first type refers to an untrue situation in the past and its probable outcome in the present; this type describes when something happens in the present, because of a particular past condition

ex) If I hadn't missed my flight, I would be in Canada now. (= In reality, I missed my flight so I am not in Canada now; a past event affects a present situation.)

3-2) The other is that the past tense is used in the ***if***-clause and then ***would (could/might) have + past participle.*** is used in the independent clause. The second type refers to an unreal situation in the present and its probable outcome in the past; this type describes when something already occurred in the past, because of a particular present condition.

ex) If we knew you were coming, we would have bought a bottle of wine yesterday. (= In reality, we don't know you are coming so we didn't buy a bottle of wine yesterday; a present situation affects a past event.)

4) ***Wish*** with a ***that***-clause can be used to express a regretful and imaginary situation. In order to represent a wish, regret, or dissatisfaction for the present or future, simple past tense

follows ***wish***; in order to represent a wish, regret or dissatisfaction for the past, past perfect aspect follows ***wish***.

ex) I wish I didn't have to go to school tomorrow.
(= In reality, I have to go to school tomorrow.)
I wish you had kept the secret.
(= In reality, you didn't keep the secret; a present regret or dissatisfaction over a past action that did not occur.)
I wished you had kept the secret. (a past regret over a past action that did not occur.)

Wish can express a desire for something that is unlikely or impossible. However, ***hope*** can state a desire for something that is more likely or possible.

ex) I wish I could go out with her.
(= I think it is almost impossible for me to go out with her; The event (going out with her) is less likely to happen to me.)
I hope I can go out with her.
(= I think it is possible for me to go out with her; The event (going out with her) is more likely to happen to me.)

5) Conditional IF vs. Hypothetical IF

5-1) For conditional ***if,*** the possibility/probability of happening is quite high and open. In other words, a present tense verb in the conditional ***if***-clause represents a cause and condition in a true situation. Therefore, an action in the main clause represents an effect and result.

ex) If Tom works hard, he will save a lot of money.
(= Tom must work hard. As a result, he can save a lot of money.)

5-2) For hypothetical ***if***, the possibility/probability of happening is quite low and poor. A past tense verb in the hypothetical ***if***-clause refers to something that is untrue or imaginary in the present or future. Therefore, an action in the main clause will or does not occur. In addition, a past perfect aspect verb in the hypothetical ***if***-clause refers to something that is untrue or imaginary in the past. As a result, an action in the main clause did not happen.

ex) If Tom worked hard, he would save a lot of money.
(= In reality, Tom doesn't work hard, so he will/does not save a lot of money.)
If Tom worked hard, he would have saved a lot of money.
(= In reality, Tom didn't work hard, so he couldn't save a lot of money.)

Exercise

Put the verbs into the correct form.

1. If I (get) the phone call, I (hear) the news.
   (= But I didn't get the phone call and I didn't hear the news.)

2. I (save) a lot of money now if I (take) that job.
   (= But I didn't take that job and I don't save a lot of money now.)

3. If I (be) stronger, I (help) him carry the table.
   (= But I am not strong and I can't help him carry the table.)

4. I wish I (have) enough money to travel to London.
   (= I don't have enough money now, and I am afraid of it because I can't go there.)

5. If he (be, not) sick, he (come) to the party.
   (= But he was sick and he didn't come to the party.)

6. If I (learn) Spanish, I (translate) the message for him.
(= In reality, I don't learn Spanish now and that is why I couldn't translate the message in the past.)

7. I wish that the bus (be) on time.
(= Unfortunately, the bus was late, and I missed an important meeting.)

8. I (buy) these gloves if they (fit).
(= But the gloves don't fit and I don't buy them.)

9. If Maria (know) the truth, she (tell) us.
(= But she didn't know the truth and she didn't tell us.)

10. I wish I (go) to college after high school.
(= Unfortunately, I didn't go to college and I couldn't get a better job.)

11. If you (follow) my advice, you (be, not) in such trouble now.
(= In reality, you didn't follow my advice so you are in trouble now.)

12. If the taxi (arrive) on time, she (not, miss) the flight.
(= But the taxi didn't arrive on time and she missed the flight.)

13. If I (not, break) my arm, I (take) part in the football match. (= But I broke my arm, and I didn't take part in the football match.)

14. The soup (taste) better if you (add) more salt. (= But you don't add more salt and the soup doesn't taste good.)

15. If Amy (be) more honest, she (admit) her faults. (= But she isn't honest and she doesn't admit her faults.)

| References |

Ahmad, N. (2011). *Error Analysis: Learning Articles and Prepositions among Secondary School Students in Pakistan. Interdisciplinary Journal of Contemporary Research in Business*, *2*, 385-391.

Akhtar, N., & Tomasello, M. (1997). Young children's productivity with word order and verb morphology. *Developmental Psychology*, *33*, 952-965.

Akhtar, N. (1999). Acquiring basic word order: evidence for data-driven learning of syntactic structure. *Journal of Child Language*, *26*, 339-356.

Altenberg, B. (1993). Recurrent verb complement constructions in the London-Lund Corpus. In J. Aarts, P. de Hann, & N. Oostdijk (Eds.), *English language corpora: design, analysis and exploitation* (pp. 227-245). Amsterdam: Rodopi.

Bachman, L. F. (1990). *Fundamental Considerations in Language Testing.* New York: Oxford University Press.

Bakeman, R., & Adamson, L. (1984). Coordinating attention to people and objects in mother-infant and peer-infant interactions. *Child Development*, *55*, 1278-1289.

Baker, C. (1979). Syntactic theory and the projection problem. *Linguistic Inquiry*, *10*, 533-581.

Barlow, M., & Kemmer, S. (2000). *Usage-based models of grammar.* Stanford, CA: CSLI Publications.

Bates, E. (1979). *The emergence of symbols: Cognition and communication in infancy*. New York: Academic Press.

Bencini, G., & Goldberg, A. (2000). The contribution of argument structure constructions to sentence meaning. *Journal of Memory and Language*, *43*, 640-651.

Bennet, D. (1975). *Spatial and Temporal uses of English Prepositions*. London: Longman.

Biber, D., Conrad, S., & Reppen, R. (1999). *Longman grammar of spoken and written English*. New York: Longman.

Biber, D., & Geoffrey L. (2002). *Student Grammar of Spoken and Written English*. London: Pearson Education Limited.

Bijon K. Sarker &Seunghyun Baek. (2016). Revisiting Fluctuations in L2 Article Choice in L1-Korean L2-English Learners.

Blake, J. B. (2008). *All About Language*. Oxford: Oxford University Press.

Boas, H. (2010). The syntax-lexicon continuum in construction grammar: A study of English communication verbs. *Belgian Journal of Linguistics*, *24*, 52-82.

Boas, H. (2013). Cognitive construction grammar. In T. Hoffmann & G. Trousdale (Eds.), *The oxford handbook of construction grammar* (pp. 15-31). Oxford: Oxford University Press.

Bolinger, D. (1968). Entailment and the meaning of structures. *Glossa*, *2*, 119-127.

Booij, G. (2010). *Construction morphology*. Oxford: Oxford University Press.

Booij, G. (2013). Morphology in construction grammar. In T. Hoffmann & G. Trousdale (Eds.), *The oxford handbook of construction grammar* (pp. 15-31). Oxford: Oxford University Press.

Bowermann, M. (1982). Reorganizational processes in lexical and syntactic development. In E. Wanner & L. R. Gleitman (Eds.), *Language acquisition: The state of the art* (pp. 319-346). New York: Cambridge University Press.

Boyd, J., & Goldberg, A. (2009). Input effects within a constructionist framework. *The Modern Language Journal*, *93*, 418-429.

Braine, M. (1976). Children's first word combinations. *Monographs of the Society for Research in Child Development*, *41*, 1 – 97.

Braine, M. (1987). What is learned in acquiring word classes: A step toward an acquisition theory. In B. MacWhinney (Ed.), *Mechanisms of language acquisition* (pp. 65-87). Hillsdale, NJ: Erlbaum.

Broccias, C. (2008). Cognitive linguistic theories of grammar and grammar teaching. In S. De Knop & T. De Rycker (Eds.), *Cognitive approaches to pedagogical grammar* (pp. 67-90). New York: Mouton de Gruyter.

Brooks, P., & Tomasello, M. (1999). How children constrain their argument structure constructions. *Language*, *75*, 720-738.

Brown, L. (ed) (1993), *The New Shorter Oxford English Dictionary*. Oxford: Clarendon Press.

Brown, H. D. (2000). *Principles of language learning and teaching (4th ed.)*. San Francisco State University: Pearson Education Limited.

Brown, H. D. (2007). *Teahing by Principle. (3rd ed.)*. Englewood Cliffs, NJ: Prentice Hall.

Bybee, J. (1985). *Morphology: A study of the relation between meaning and form*. Amsterdam: Benjamins.

Bybee, J., & Pagliuca, W. (1994). *The evolution of grammar: Tense, aspect and modality in the languages of the world*. Chicago: University of Chicago Press.

Bybee, J. (2001). *Phonology and language use*. Cambridge: Cambridge University Press.

Bybee, J., & Hopper, P. (2001). Introduction to frequency and the emergence of linguistic structure. In J. Bybee & P. Hopper (Eds.), *Frequency and the emergence of linguistic structure* (pp. 1-24). Amsterdam: John Benjamins.

Bybee, J. (2006). From usage to grammar: The mind's response to repetition. *Language*, *82*, 711-733.

Bybee, J. (2013). Usage-based theory and exemplar representations of constructions. In T. Hoffmann & G. Trousdale (Eds.), *The oxford handbook of construction grammar* (pp. 49-69). Oxford: Oxford University Press.

Cameron-Faulkner, T., Lieven, E., & Tomasello, M. (2003). A constructionbased analysis of child-directed speech. *Cognitive Science*, *27*, 843-873.

Canale, M., & Swain, M. (1980). Theoretical bases of communicative approaches to second language teaching and testing. *Applied Linguistics*, *1*, 1-47.

Casenhiser, D., & Goldberg, A. (2005). Fast mapping of a phrasal form and meaning. *Developmental Science*, *8*, 500-508.

Celce, M. (1991). Grammar pedagogy in second and foreign language teaching. *TESOL Quarterly*, *25*, 459-480.

Celce, M. & Diane, L. (1999). *The grammar book: An ESL/EFL teachers' Course (Second edition)*. Newsbury: Heinle & Heinle Publishers.

Chafe, W. (1994). *Discourse, consciousness and time: The flow and displacement of conscious experience in speaking and writing*. Chicago: University of Chicago Press.

Chomsky, N. (1965). *Aspects of the theory of syntax*. Cambridge: MIT Press.

Chomsky, N. (1981). *Lectures on government and binding*. Dordrecht: Foris.

Chomsky, N. (1986). *Knowledge of language: Its nature, origin, and use*. New York: Praeger.

Clark, E. (1987). The principle of contrast: A constraint on language acquisition. In B. MacWhinney (Ed.), *Mechanisms of language acquisition* (pp. 1 - 33). Hillsdale, NJ: Lawrence Erlbaum Associates.

Clark, H. (1996). *Using language*. Cambridge: Cambridge University Press.

Close, R. A. (1981). *English as a Foreign Language: Its Constant Grammatical Problems*. London: George Allen and Unwin.

Collins, L., Trofimovich, P., White, J., Cardoso, W., & Horst, M. (2009). Some input on the easy/difficult grammar question: An empirical study. *The Modern Language Journal*, *93*, 336-353.

Conway, C., & Christiansen, M. (2001). Sequential learning in non-human primates. *Trends in Cognitive Sciences*, *5*, 529-546.

Corder, P. (1967). The significance of learners errors. *International Review of Applied Linguistics*, *5*, 161-169.

Corkum, V., & Moore, C. (1995). Development of joint visual attention in infants. In C. Moore & P. Dunham (Eds.), *Joint attention: Its origins and role in development* (pp. 61-83). Hillsdale, NJ: Erlbaum.

Cowan, R. (2008). *The Teacher's Grammar of English: A Course Book and Reference Guide*. Cambridge: Cambridge University Press.

Croft, W. (2013). Radical construction grammar. In T. Hoffmann & G. Trousdale (Eds.), *The oxford handbook of construction grammar* (pp. 15-31). Oxford: Oxford University Press.

Culicover, P., & Jackendoff, R. (2005). *Simpler Syntax*. Oxford: Oxford University Press.

Curme. (1935). *A Grammar of the English Language - Vol. 3. II. Parts of Speech Accidence*. Boston: D.C Heath & Company.

Dabrowksa, E. (2004). *Language, mind, and brain: Some psychological and neurological constraints on theories of grammar*. Edinburgh: Edinburgh University Press.

Dash, N., & Dash, M. (2007). *Teaching English as an Additional Language*. New Delhi: Atlantic Publishers & Distributors (P) Ltd.

DeKeyser, R. (2003). Implicit and explicit learning. In C. Doughty & M. Long (Eds.), *Handbook of second language learning* (pp.313-348). Oxford: Blackwell.

Dodson, K., & Tomasello, M. (1998). Acquiring the transitive construction in English: The role of animacy and pronouns. *Journal of Child Language*, *25*, 605-622.

Dörnyei, Z. (2009). *The psychology of second language acquisition*. Oxford: Oxford University Press.

Dulay, H., & Burt, M. (1973). Should we teach children syntax? *Language Learning*, *23*, 245-258.

Dulay, H., & Burt, M. (1974). Natural sequence in child second language acquisition. *Language Learning*, *24*, 37-53.

Dulay, H., Burt, M., & Krashen, S. (1982). *Language two*. New York: Oxford University Press.

Eastwood, J. (2002). *Oxford Practice Grammar*. Oxford: Oxford University Press.

Ellis, R. (1993). The structural syllabus and second language acquisition. *TESOL Quarterly*, *27*, 91-113.

Ellis, R. (2002). *The Study of Second Language Acquisition*. New York: Oxford University Press.

Ellis, R. (2006). Current issues in the teaching of grammar: An SLA perspective. *TESOL Quarterly*, *40*, 83-107.

Felix, S. W. (1985). More evidence on competing cognitive systems. *Second Language Research*, *1*, 47-72.

Finer, D., & Broselow, E. (1986). Second language acquisition of reflexive binding. *Proceedings of NELS*, *16*, 154-168.

Fitikides, T. J. (2002). *Common Mistakes in English*. London: Pearson Education Limited.

Flynn, S. (1987). *A Parameter-Setting Model of L2 Acquisition*. Dordrecht: Reidel.

Flynn, S., & Martohardjono, G. (1994). Mapping from the initial state to the final state: the separation of universal principles and language specific properties. *Syntactic Theory and First Language Acquisition: Crosslinguistic Perspectives*, *1*, 319-335.

Fujimori, A., Yoshimura, N, Nakayama, M., Sawasaki, K, & Takeda, S. (2013) Acquisition of English perfectives by Japanese adult learners. *Ars Linguistica, 20*, 62-72.

Funk., & Wagnalls. (1953). *Prepositions, Conjunctions, Relative Pronouns and Adverbs*. New York: Funk & Wagnalls Company.

Heaton, J. B. (1995), *Prepositions and Adverbial Particles*. Essex: Longman.

Hewings, M. (1999). *Advanced Grammar in Use: A self-study reference and practice book for advanced learners of English*. Cambridge: Cambridge University Press.

Hoffman, S. (2005). *Grammaticalization and English Complex Prepositions: A Corpus Based Study*. New York: Routledge.

Hornby, A. S. (1974). *Oxford Advanced Learner's Dictionary of Current Language*. Oxford: Oxford University Press.

Ionin, T. (2006). This is definitely specific: specificity and definiteness in article systems. *Natural Language Semantics, 14*, 175-234.

Ionin, T., Ko, H., & Wexler, K. (2004). Article semantics in L2 acquisition: the role of specificity. *Language Acquisition, 12*, 3-69.

Ionin, T., Zubizarreta, M. L., & Maldonado, S. B. (2008). Sources of linguistic knowledge in the second language acquisition of English articles. *Lingua, 118*, 554-576.

Kenndy, G. (2003). *Structure and Meaning in English: A Guide for Teachers*. London: Pearson Education Limited.

Krashen, S. (1981). *Second Language Acquisition and Second Language Learning*. Oxford: Pergamon Press.

Langer, J. A. (1986). Learning through writing: Study skills in the content areas. *Journal of Reading, 29,* 400-406.

Long, M. H. (1983). Does second language instruction make a difference? A review of research. *TESOL Quarterly*, *17*, 359-382.

Long, M. H. (1991). *Focus on form: A design feature in language teaching methodology*. Amsterdam: Jon Benjamins.

Lunn, P. (1987). *The semantics of por and para*. Bloomington: Indiana University Linguistics Club.

Lyons, J. (1981). *Language and Linguistics: An Introduction.* Cambridge: Cambridge University Press.

Manchon, R. M. (2011). *Learning-to-Write and Writing-to-Learn in an Additional Language*. Amsterdam: John Benjamins Publishing Company.

McGinley, W., & Tierney, R. J. (1989). Traversing the topical landscape: Reading and writing as ways of knowing. *Written Communication,* 6, 243-269.

Murphy, R. (2004). *English Grammar in Use*. Cambridge: Cambridge University Press.

Narayanaswamy, K. R. (2004). *A Teacher's Grammar of English*. Chennai: Orient Longman Pvt. Ltd.

Patel, M. F & Jain, P. M. (2008). *English Language Teaching: Methods, Tools & Techniques*. Jaipur: Sunrise Publishers & Distributors.

Pittman, G. A. (1966). *Activating the use of prepositions*. London: Longman Green and Co, Ltd.

Pullum, G. K., & Scholz, B. C. (2002). Empirical assessment of stimulus poverty arguments. *The linguistic Review*, *18*, 9-50.

Roberts, P. (1954). *Understanding Grammar*. New York: Harper and Row Publishers Incorporates.

Richards, J. (1991). *The Context of Language Teaching*. London: University Press.

Sarker, B., & Baek, S. (2017). Revisiting Fluctuations in L2 Article Choice in L1-Korean L2-English Learners. *Journal of Psycholinguistics Research, 46(2),* 367-393.

Schumacher, G. M., & Gradwohl Nash, J. (1991). Conceptualizing and measuring knowledge change due to writing. *Research in the Teaching of English, 25,* 67-96.

Schwartz, B. D. (1992). Testing between UG-based and problem-solving models of L2A: developmental sequence data. *Language Acquisition*, *2*, 1-19.

Schwartz, B. D., & Sprouse, R. A. (1996). L2 cognitive states and the full transfer/full access model. *Second Language Research*, *12*, 40-72.

Selinker, L. (1972). Interlanguage. *IRAL-International Review of Applied Linguistics in Language Teaching, 10*, 209-232.

Selinker, L., Swain, M., & Dumas, G. (1975). The Interlanguage hypothesis extended to children 1. *Language Learning*, *25*, 139-152.

Sinclair, J. (ed) (1992), *Collins Cobuild English Grammar*. London: Harper Collins.

Sinha, H. S. (2000). *English Language and Linguistics*. Jaipur: Mangal Deep Publications.

Spada, N., & Lightbown, P. (1993). Instruction and the development of questions in L2 classrooms. *Studies in Second Language Acquisition*, *15*, 205-241.

Strang, B. (1962). *Modern English Structure*. London: Edward Arnold Publishers Ltd.

Swan, M. (2005). *Practical English Usage*. Oxford: Oxford University Press.

Takahaski, G. (1969). Perceptions of space and function of certain English prepositions. *Language Learning, 10*, 217-234.

Thomson, A. J & Martinet, A. V. (1986). *A Practical English Grammar.* New York: Oxford University Press.

Thomason, T., & Geoff W. (2009). *Tools Not Rules: Teaching Grammar in the Writing Classroom*. Durham: Eloquent Books Ltd.

Thomas, P. E. (2011). *Understanding English Grammar*. Cambridge: Cambridge University Press.

Thornbury, S. (1999). *How to teach grammar*. Harlow: Longman.

Tyler, A., & Evans, V. (2003). *The Semantics of English Prepositions: Spatial Scenes, Embodied Meaning and Cognition.* Cambridge: Cambridge University Press.

Valenzuela, J., & Rojo, A. (2008). What can language learners tell us about constructions? In S. Knop & R. Rycker (Eds.), *Cognitive approaches to pedagogical grammar* (pp. 198-230). Berlin: Mouton de Gruyter.

Viberg, A. (2002) Basic verbs in second language acquisition. *Revue Françcaise de Linguistique Appliquéee*, *2*, 61-79.

Walker, R. H. (1967). Teaching the present perfect tenses. *Tesol Quarterly*, *1*, 17-30.

Weist, R. M., Wysocka, H., & Lyytinen, P. (1991). Across-linguistic perspective on the development of temporal systems. *Journal of Child Language*, *18*, 67-92.

Wexler, K., & Chien, Y. C. (1985). The development of lexical anaphors and pronouns. *Papers and Reports on Child Language Development*, *24*, 138-149.

Wexler, K., & Culicover, P. (1980). Formal principles of language acquisition. *Language*, *58*, 413-421.

White, L. (1982). *Grammatical Theory and Language Acquisition.* Dordrecht: Foris.

White, L. (1996). Clitics in L2 French. *Language Acquisition and Language Disorders*, *14*, 335-368.

Wierzbicka, A. (1980). *Lingua mentalis: the semantics of natural language*. New York: Academic Press.

Wierzbicka, A. (1988). *The semantics of grammar*. Amsterdam: John Benjamins.

Wilson, S. (2003). Lexically-specific constructions in the acquisition of inflection in English. *Journal of Child Language*, *30*, 75-115.

Wittek, A., & Tomasello, M. (2005). German-speaking children's productivity with syntactic constructions and case morphology: Local cues help locally. *First Language*, *25*, 103-125.

Woodall, B. R. (2002). Language-switching: using the first language while writing in a second language. *Journal of Second Language Writing*, *11*, 7-28.

Year, J., & Gordon, P. (2009). Korean speakers' acquisition of the English ditransitive construction: the role of verb prototype, input distribution, and frequency. *The Modern Language Journal*, *93*, 399-417.

Zobl, H. (1980). The formal and developmental selectivity of L1 influence on L2 acquisition. *Language Learning*, *30*, 43-57.